I Have Seen the *Kingdom*

A Revelation of
God's Final Glory

 Kingsley
Fletcher

with J. Nelson Black, Ph.D.

Char
HO
Books about Sp

I HAVE SEEN THE KINGDOM by Kingsley Fletcher
with J. Nelson Black, Ph.D.
Published by Charisma House
A part of Strang Communications Company
600 Rinehart Road
Lake Mary, Florida 32746
www.charismahouse.com

This book or parts thereof may not be reproduced in any form, stored in a retrieval system, or transmitted in any form by any means—electronic, mechanical, photocopy, recording, or otherwise—without prior written permission of the publisher, except as provided by United States of America copyright law.

Unless otherwise noted, all Scripture quotations are from the New King James Version of the Bible. Copyright © 1979, 1980, 1982 by Thomas Nelson, Inc., publishers. Used by permission.

Scripture quotations marked KJV are from the King James Version of the Bible.

Scripture quotations marked RSV are from the Revised Standard Version of the Bible. Copyright © 1946, 1952, 1971 by the Division of Christian Education of the National Council of the Churches of Christ in the USA. Used by permission.

Scripture quotations marked NIV are from the Holy Bible, New International Version. Copyright © 1973, 1978, 1984, International Bible Society. Used by permission.

Scripture quotations marked TLB are from The Living Bible, Copyright © 1971. Used by permission of Tyndale House Publishers, Inc., Wheaton, IL 60189. All rights reserved.

Scripture quotations marked NLT are from the Holy Bible, New Living Translation, Copyright © 1996. Used by permission of Tyndale House Publishers, Inc., Wheaton, IL 60189. All rights reserved.

Copyright © 1998 by Kingsley Fletcher
All rights reserved

Library of Congress Cataloging-in-Publication Data:
Fletcher, Kingsley A.
      I have seen the Kingdom / Kingsley Fletcher.
        p. cm.
      ISBN: 0–88419–485–X (pbk.)
        1. Kingdom of God. 2. Christian life. I. Title.
BT94.F57 1998
231.7'2—dc21
                                    98-5866
                                        CIP

Printed in the United States of America
01 02 03 04   7 6 5 4 3 2

Dedication

I dedicate this book to my father, Jacob, a precious chief (king) who has taught me to understand the principles of kingship. The things you taught me have become the backbone of my life and ministry.

I was honored to be called into the presence of my father and his twin brother, Isaac, in their old age and have them lay their hands on me and bless me and bless my seed and the future generations. I am privileged for the opportunity of knowing how to be a king—both in the natural and in the spiritual.

I dedicate this book also to my mother, Esther Victoria, a woman with less Western influence but one who is full of the wisdom of God. My father taught me how to come to God—but my mother taught me how to speak to God. My father taught me discipline—my mother taught me sensitivity to the things of God. My parents are the best mentors anyone could have.

I also dedicate this book to Martha, my loving wife, and to our daughters—Anna-Kissel and Damaris Joy—and my adopted sons—Teddy, Abiy, and Addisu—for being blessings to me and true reflections of the kingdom.

Acknowledgments

I want to take this time to acknowledge some of my closest friends, including Myles Munroe, Tom Winters, Bart Pierce, Laurie Beth Jones, Carlton Arthurs, Randy Morrison, Garth Coonce, Darrell Hines, Tommy Tenney, and Steve Munsey. Thank you for your support, friendship, and encouragement.

There are many others who mean so much to me. It would be impossible to name each one of you, but remember, you are at the top of the list for my next book.

Thank you to my dear friends in ministry around the world who have allowed me to share my life and ministry with them.

I want to acknowledge Jim Nelson Black, my wonderful editor and friend, for his extraordinary ability to work with me on this book.

And thank you to all people, believers and nonbelievers alike, who are seeking for truth and are open to biblical principles. May His kingdom be a reality for each one of you.

Contents

For unto us a Child is born,
Unto us a Son is given;
And the government will be upon His shoulder.
And His name will be called
Wonderful, Counselor, Mighty God,
Everlasting Father, Prince of Peace.
Of the increase of His government and peace
There will be no end,
Upon the throne of David and over His kingdom,
To order it and establish it with judgment and justice
From that time forward, even forever.
The zeal of the LORD of hosts will perform this.

—ISAIAH 9:6–7

Part I:
The Words of the King

1

Lift Up Your Heads

CHRISTIANITY TODAY is influenced by the West more than is good for us. Our ideas about equality, tolerance, and authority that have infiltrated the church through the democratic institutions of the West over the past two hundred years have influenced how we think about our relationships with God. As a result, Christians today have no true understanding of what a kingdom is all about. And we have little knowledge and even less discernment of the kingdom of God.

Many people, because of the political and cultural views of our society, believe that Christianity is a democracy where everyone is equal and gets a vote. That is precisely the opposite of reality. Even though God created man equal, He gave individual gifts, abilities, and callings. With every gift, ability, and calling there is responsibility. We are equal in God—but unequal in terms of our responsibilities.

The kingdom of God is—and always shall be—a majestic realm, a great and powerful empire, a monarchy, and a royal dominion that demands absolute loyalty to the King. Every subject must be willing to give his or her life for the King. That's how a monarchy works, and the kingdom of heaven is the greatest monarchy of all time. But that is the opposite of what most people believe.

In this book I will examine how this erroneous belief came about and what we must do to correct it. To the discussion I bring my own experience and witness as the son of a chief [king] born into

1

royalty, heir to a throne, raised to enjoy all the privileges of an earthly kingdom in Ghana, West Africa, and called out of Africa by God to be a missionary to the people of the West.

I will also mention certain aspects of my own background, especially my travels, long periods of residence in many countries, and the two hundred thirty-five churches I have had the privilege of planting and pastoring in various places around the world. Most of all I want to use my background and experience to take a closer look at the kingdom of God today and how, through faulty teaching and confusion brought about by our political, religious, and social institutions, we have lost sight of the Bible's teachings about the kingdom.

We have come such a long way from the biblical view of God's kingdom that we've lost touch with reality. But if the church of Jesus Christ expects to prepare men and women for the Second Coming of their Messiah—which we believe will be soon—then we had better start teaching them now how to honor Him as Lord and King. How we understand our role today has everything to do with our fitness to serve the King of glory when He establishes His eternal kingdom on earth. (See Revelation 5:10.)

HOLY HOUSEKEEPING

BEFORE WE CAN come into the presence of a just and holy God, however, we must throw out a lot of bad ideas, a lot of faulty thinking, and defective emotions. Our feelings about God and His rightful place in our lives must change. We need to do a little holy housekeeping.

No one whose heart is cluttered with knickknacks of bad ideas and worn-out theology can give our eternal sovereign Lord all the dignity, honor, praise, and glory He deserves. No one who holds back from giving true obedience to Him can ever be a subject of the King.

That's what this book is about. Because we do not understand the kingdom, we see the sovereign Lord and Redeemer of all mankind merely as our friend, and not more. We make Him our example, but we do not honor Him as master, ruler, and King. Because we have little knowledge of the kingdom, we see Jesus as a sort of celestial sidekick. He's our pal. Yes, we see Him as a Savior, but we fail to recognize Him as the Christ, the Lord, and the only begotten Son of God who "shall judge between many peoples, and rebuke strong nations" (Mic. 4:3).

For the last two hundred years, the church's attitude toward Jesus Christ has been on its own terms. But now we must see Him with new eyes. We must see Jesus not only as Savior and Redeemer, but also as the King, the Sovereign, the most high God, and the One who must be obeyed in all things.

Jesus is our friend, but it is vitally important to understand that it was He who offered His friendship to us. In John 15:15–16 we read, "No longer do I call you servants, for a servant does not know what his master is doing; but I have called you friends, for all things that I heard from My Father I have made known to you. You did not choose Me, but I chose you."

The one who initiates friendship often offers more—and our lives are more enriched by that friendship. Our friend Jesus has enriched our lives beyond measure. Yet we often exploit the goodness of our Redeemer by failing to give His friendship to us the honor and reverence it demands. We say, "Since Jesus is our friend, surely He will not be offended by our constant failures, quibbles, and private sins."

And it doesn't stop there. When we present Him to people, we don't present Him as Christ, the Lord and King of all creation, but merely as Jesus, our heavenly buddy. Because we don't see Him in His true position as Lord of lords and King of kings, it is difficult for us to approach the throne of grace with reverence and honor. We have not truly recognized that Jesus Christ is the one and only gateway to God.

Though He is God revealed in human flesh, Jesus is also the Ruler who tells us that we have to obey Him. But because we do not know Him as our King, we don't really obey Him as we should. We say, "Lord! Lord!", but we fail to do as He demands. We don't take up our cross daily and follow Him. We are not occupying the world and conquering the darkness in His name. We do not live each day as He demands.

Like the ancient Pharisees, we prefer to give Him convenient and painless sacrifices when, in fact, what He really wants is personal obedience. The Word of God tells us that obedience is better than sacrifice (1 Sam. 15:22). When you serve the King, put down your sacrifice and obey the King. If you wish to live in the kingdom, you must do whatever the King requires and says.

The results of misunderstanding and disobedience can be seen in our world—even in the crumbling condition of Christianity. All over the world, women and men who call themselves Christians meet together to determine if the language of the Bible should be changed to reflect modern-day lifestyles. Some people want to "reimagine" the meaning of God, stripping away parts of our Christian doctrines that "interfere" with their autonomy and "rights."

Where are the faithful servants of the King? The King never gave anyone the authority to question His kingship. Surely sin and shame accrue to us when we tolerate such behavior in the church of Jesus Christ. And yet, that is not even the worst part.

The church right now is full of recycling. We recycle everything. Everyone is eating from the same pot. However, we're not reaching the people we've been sent to reach. Instead, we sit comfortably in our air-conditioned, stained-glass-windowed sanctuaries and expect them to come to us. But the King's command is very simple: "Go therefore and make disciples of all the nations, baptizing them in the name of the Father and of the Son and of the Holy Spirit, teaching them to observe all things that I have commanded you" (Matt. 28:19–20).

We are commanded to go into the fields and harvest for Him. If we do that, He says, then, "I am with you always, even to the end of the age" (Matt. 28:20). Please notice that He is with us only if we keep His commands. If we fail to obey, the King will not reward us. He will not give us our wages. He will not allow us to take His commandments for granted.

Because we see Him only as a friend instead of as our King, we treat Him as we choose. After all, we have our "rights," don't we? So we treat our King according to our feelings at any given moment. We choose what we want, do as we please, and give Him our scraps and leftovers when we're done. But please believe me, you do not do that with a king.

What makes a king kingly is his power and his glory. The king has the highest standing in the kingdom. What comes out of his kingdom represents his power. What the king says is power. When we honor the king, we manifest his glory. But if we fail to recognize the king in his power and glory, then we are not fit subjects of the king.

A CONFLICT OF CULTURES

THE BIBLE WAS written at a time and in a culture as different as possible from our culture today. It was written for people who understood order and authority in a way that the world today no longer remembers. Those who first read the Scriptures lived under the rule of kings—and knew what it meant to respect their king. But in our modern-day democracies we have forgotten how to respect anyone in authority—not only kings, but government officials, law enforcement officers, public servants, teachers, church leaders, and even our own parents.

We no longer respect our president or political leaders. If we cannot respect and honor those in democratically elected positions of authority—people we see with our own eyes—then how can we honor the great and eternal King whom we have not seen? If we no longer honor God or man, how will we ever hear the words of teachers, pastors, and prophets of the King?

I fear we turn off more people through our insolence and bad behavior than we turn on to Jesus Christ. Many people look at the anarchy and disorder so prevalent in today's society and say, "If that's their idea of order and peace, then I want none of it." They look at the ways we do violence to the name of Jesus Christ and the disrespect with which people in the Christian culture treat the sovereignty of God. They say, "If that's how Christians feel about their God, then I want none of it!"

Are we responsible for the souls of those who are offended and lost for eternity because of our bad examples? In some ways, I fear we may be. We seem to go out of our way to revise, change, or ignore anything about the Christian faith that makes us the least bit uncomfortable.

I Have Seen the Kingdom

We want to change the whole world to be more like us culturally. Look at the way Westerners behave when traveling abroad. We try to change people's culture from the outside without teaching them that God demands that our hearts and minds be transformed from the inside. Our King desires to change His people's nature to reflect the Spirit and glory of His kingdom.

If an earthly king is a true king, not only will his people trust him, praise him, and appreciate him, but they will also speak well of him. But look at how we treat our God and King. We are the only people in the world who treat our God with discontent. We are the only people who have the audacity to say to our God, "I'm mad at You!" But what right do we have to be mad at our King?

The Bible tells us to stay at our post when the king is angry. "If the spirit of the ruler rises against you, do not leave your post; for conciliation pacifies great offenses" (Eccles. 10:4). We do not have the freedom to leave the presence of our King when He is angry with us. We need to humble ourselves before the King, seek His favor, and be reconciled to Him. While our human freedom permits us to speak our mind or walk away when we are displeased with a situation, we cannot speak our mind or walk away when the King is displeased with us. Unfortunately, the Western world has no concept of these things.

Consider how few hours we spend before the Lord. When we make petitions before Him, we do it on our own terms, based on what we feel or don't feel. We hold the King responsible for meeting our needs and satisfying our demands. If we don't get immediate results, we get upset with Him and say, "The King is silent or forgetful or powerless." Jesus is not obligated to people in His kingdom who have no regard for Him.

The modern church has given herself the right to resist her heavenly King and even to be rude to Him. How many times have you heard someone say, "If you're upset with God, don't be shy. Tell Him that you are upset with Him."

To me, one who has been raised by a king, that is shocking! Such an action shows no regard for the awesome majesty and glory of our King. This is no ordinary sovereign: He is the King of the universe! We cannot treat God like a celestial errand boy! He is not an errand boy. He is our God and Master. Bow before Him. *He is our King*—the One to whom our fathers bowed down (Exod. 34:8).

When Daniel found himself in the presence of God's messenger, his knees buckled under him, he turned pale, and he fell on his face in the dirt!

Listen to the words of the prophet:

> I, Daniel, was the only one who saw the vision; the men with me did not see it, but such terror overwhelmed them that they fled and hid themselves. So I was left alone, gazing at this great vision; I had no strength left, my face turned deathly pale and I was helpless. Then I heard him speaking, and as I listened to him, I fell into a deep sleep, my face to the ground. A hand touched me and set me trembling on my hands and knees.
> —DANIEL 10:7–10, NIV

Finding himself in the presence of the majesty of God, Daniel did what any rational human being would do: He hit the pavement! And, believe me, you would to the same thing in that situation!

We talk back to the King. We say, "King, I don't want what You offer. You'll have to change it for me to make me happy, because that's Your job—making sure that I'm happy most of the time." Or we tell Him, "Jesus, You've got to get off my back! You're getting too close. You're demanding too much of me!" Unbelievable! Such effrontery in the face of the King of the universe!

FRUIT OF THE SPIRIT

THE GREATEST SIN of the West today is not pornography, violence, marital infidelity, or any of the issues about which we are rightly concerned, even though they are abhorrent to God. Our greatest sin is the sin of **pride** (spiritual, natural, material, and racial) that has allowed a spirit of unthankfulness and impertinence to grow up in our hearts.

Obviously, we have never truly appreciated what God has done for us. God was trying to establish—in this land and upon these shores—a society that could be a replica of what the kingdom of

God is supposed to be. He wanted this land to be "a city that is set on a hill" (Matt. 5:14, KJV). But over time we have taken God's favor for granted and have lost the spirit of thankfulness. When people lose thankfulness, they also lose patience. No wonder so many Christians have lost their peace, joy, and security in Christ.

Remember the fruit of the Spirit? "Love, joy, peace, patience, kindness, goodness, faithfulness, gentleness and self-control. Against such things," says Paul, "there is no law" (Gal. 5:22–23, NIV). We seem to be saying that since there is no law *against* them, there is no law *for* them either. Perhaps there should be a law against the rejection of them, for they are truly the attributes of a mature Christian faith.

If we are thankful to the King, we will always praise Him. We will talk about His goodness and generosity, with words of praise pouring forth from our mouths. The news of the goodness of the King should fill the land. But most of the time we are silent about our great God and King. For many of us, one hour on Sunday is the best we can offer, and we sleep through most of that.

This is a society that, rather than serving as a model of the heavenly kingdom, has become a model of arrogance, thanklessness, self-indulgence, and pride. There is no better evidence that we are approaching the End Times than the hardness of our hearts. Hear these words of Paul:

> But mark this: There will be terrible times in the last days. People will be lovers of themselves, lovers of money, boastful, proud, abusive, disobedient to their parents, ungrateful, unholy, without love, unforgiving, slanderous, without self-control, brutal, not lovers of the good, treacherous, rash, conceited, lovers of pleasure rather than lovers of God—having a form of godliness but denying its power.
> —2 TIMOTHY 3:1–5, NIV

Does that sound like the world today? Could there be any better description of the angry, slanderous, out-of-control world of our day? And the church is not living above all this—we are right in the middle of it. In fact, a lot of the time we are the ringleaders of it, with "a form of godliness but denying its power."

We treat the God of Abraham—whom we serve—with discontent. We treat the Lord Jesus Christ like a holy errand boy. We say, "I want a bigger house or a better car. Get me a new job or a better group of friends. Hop to it, Jesus." Then we cry out impatiently, "So, what are You waiting for?"

We've got a big surprise coming, however, because Jesus is the King; no king ever takes orders from his servants. He is free from labor; He never works—He rules! That is the prerogative of a king. That's what a king does. Jesus did not take His throne to become an errand boy. Far too many Christians think that when we pray and ask the Father for something in Jesus' name, He will do everything we ask—no matter how worthless the request. They picture Jesus frantically running around trying to make sure everyone is happy!

That's absurd! We need to be taught a new sense of awe and reverence for our God. We need to understand just how royal, righteous, and resplendent He truly is. We must learn from the beginning how to understand His kingdom and how to respect the courts and the dignity of our King.

There is no doubt that democracy has been a good thing for the free world. Democracy really spurs the economy. Democracy helps those at the bottom of society to rise. But democracy has nothing to do with our spiritual lives. If anything at all, democracy saturates us with a notion of the "free market" spirit, and we somehow assume this is what the kingdom of God is like. But God says, "Your example of democracy is not what the kingdom is all about."

Peter told Jesus, "We have left all we had to follow you!" (Luke 18:28, NIV), and he was about to say, "So, now, Jesus, what are we going to get?" But Jesus preempted him and said that everyone who follows Him faithfully will receive what he deserves, many times over.

Jesus was saying, "You are in My kingdom, and I want to make sure that those in My kingdom are taken care of. Don't worry about what you're going to eat or drink or what you're going to wear. That's what consumes those who are intoxicated with this world. But you are in *My* kingdom, and I am not a poor king. I am not a king who takes no delight in his subjects. I am not a king who is interested only in his kingdom."

I Have Seen the Kingdom

Jesus also said that He is going to make us kings and priests who can approach the throne: "In My kingdom I want you to become kings and priests so that you will know how to approach the throne. When you come, you can also approach the throne with confidence. Don't throw away your confidence, which is also faith. But when I come back to establish My kingdom, will I find faith on earth? I want My people to understand that I am their King, but I do not plan to rule by Myself. I intend for you to rule with Me. I am King of all kings, and my people shall be unto me kings and priests."

THE KING'S JUDGMENT

WHEN THE PEOPLE started building the tower of Babel, they said to themselves, "Come, let us build ourselves a city, with a tower that reaches to the heavens, so that we may make a name for ourselves and not be scattered over the face of the whole earth" (Gen. 11:4, NIV). They were determined to do something, so they said, "We'll make bricks, bake them thoroughly, and when we erect the tower we will *make for ourselves a name.*" That got God's attention. In fact, Scripture makes it clear that God was troubled by what He saw in the nature of man at that moment.

You see, the Father would never do anything independently of the Son and the Holy Spirit. The Holy Spirit would never do anything independently of the Son, because the Son of God is the Word. And the Holy Spirit would never do anything independently of God the Father, because He exists to glorify the Father and to do the work of the Father and the Son. Therefore, the three holy personalities of the Trinity said to one another, "Let Us go down and see what they're building." When the Lord saw it, He said, "These people are determined to build themselves a kingdom." But there is only one kingdom that God will recognize.

The kingdom of God has already been planned. In the Book of Revelation we read, "The kingdom of the world has become the kingdom of our Lord and of his Christ, and he will reign for ever and ever" (Rev. 11:15, NIV). These words, which are sung with such spectacular beauty in Handel's *Messiah,* declare the glory of that heavenly kingdom. God's kingdom takes precedence over every other kingdom; His kingdom is eternal. Even now we are working to fulfill God's design for His kingdom.

When God saw that the men of Babylon had their hearts set on building another kingdom in which they would glorify themselves instead of God, He said, "If as one people speaking the same language they have begun to do this, then nothing they plan to do will be impossible for them" (Gen. 11:6, NIV). So the Lord went down and disturbed the language of the people so that they could no longer speak to one another and be easily understood.

God was not being cruel; rather, He wanted to make sure that the focus of men's hearts would be on the kingdom of God rather than the kingdom of men. This is explained more clearly in Acts 17, where Paul spoke to the rulers of the Greeks at the Areopagus. He says:

> From one man he [God] made every nation of men, that they should inhabit the whole earth; and he determined the times set for them and the exact places where they should live. God did this so that men would seek him and perhaps reach out for him and find him, though he is not far from each one of us. For in him we live and move and have our being.
> —ACTS 17:26–28, NIV

God will not be without a witness. He will always have one somewhere. If a nation or a people refuse to seek Him, there will be others who will. A kingdom will not flourish without people to serve the king, so God is looking for a people who will honor Him, serve Him, and bring glory and praise to His name. He takes His kingdom very seriously. Anything that disrupts His kingdom He eventually removes to make sure that His kingdom shall always remain strong, intact, and thriving.

The Western church has not always kept the teaching and building of the gospel of the kingdom as its primary focus. Instead, she attempted to transform the culture and way of life of her converts—here and abroad—into something that was alien and unnatural. Too many times missionaries and preachers have seemed to be more interested in changing the outer man than transforming the inner man.

I Have Seen the Kingdom

The modern church has even distorted the image of Jesus Christ and His kingdom. The true image of Christ—that of a Middle Eastern Jew, stripped naked, nailed to a terrible wooden scaffold with iron spikes, broken, bleeding, and hanging there before a howling, cursing, spitting, mocking crowd in absolute agony—is too horrible for most of us to face today. Yet the sight of Jesus hanging there on the cross was so revolting that even His closest friends and followers ran away and hid their eyes. Only His mother and His most trusted disciples could bear to stay with Him to the bitter end. We want to think of our Savior otherwise. But, I'm sorry to say, that's the way it was.

TURNING THINGS AROUND

IF WE WOULD look more deeply, read the Scriptures more carefully, and challenge the false images we've been given, we would gain a much greater reverence for our Lord. We would also see that not only have we accepted a false image of Jesus Christ, but we have accepted a false image of each other. This is where a large part of today's racial division comes from. This is another aspect of the image problem I want to further explore in the following chapters.

When we live in ignorance, we are controlled by distrust. We replace discernment with distrust. We suspect each other because we have not taken the time to get to know each other, and a great gulf of social and racial division has formed between us.

But there is something else that must be examined, and that is the effect of democracy when it invades the church.

Democracy can at times give us a false sense of stability, of "all-rightness" about the issues we are facing today—both within the world and within the church. When we allow our ideas about political institutions to determine the context of our faith, we distort God's plan. We say, "Well, sure, I know we've got an image problem, but it'll be okay. Everything will take care of itself, and we'll be okay if we just ignore these problems a little longer."

Do we really believe that a group of people trapped in a burning building will be saved if we just ignore their problem? Or that a country being torn apart by racial division will be okay if we just act as if the problem doesn't exist? No follower of Christ worthy of his or her salt would dare to take such a risk! We don't want to get out of our comfort zones, but the root of the problem is denial. And denial is self-imposed insanity! These problems are very real, and they won't go away by themselves.

I am a pastor, born in Africa, with a desire to know God and a burning vision from God to come to the West as a missionary. When I felt God speaking to my heart, I asked Him many times, "Lord, what in the world am I going to teach a Western, Anglo-Saxon, Christian culture? What news could I possibly bring from the churches in Africa that these people don't know already?"

I realized that the people of the West already had an image of me in their minds, and they had already defined my role before I even got here! I also realized, though, that they were mostly ignorant of my culture and traditions. All they knew of my people was what they had seen in books or on some PBS documentary. These assertions they would automatically deny. They didn't want any more bad news, especially from me. But God wouldn't listen to my excuses. He said, "Go, and teach My people in the Western world what the kingdom of God is like."

So, my message is very simple. *I have seen the kingdom.* I have lived in the household of a king. I may yet serve as king of my own people someday, should I decide to accept the inheritance of my father and of our traditions as king-makers. Yes, I understand and appreciate so well all that the West has done for me and my people; but, very simply, God has sent me as an ambassador of His kingdom to the Western church.

I am a missionary from the kingdom of God, sent by the King to say that if we want to be a part of His kingdom, then we must change our way of thinking. Why? Because our way of thinking about the King of glory will not survive in the kingdom of heaven toward which we are racing at this very hour. Will you come back to the Word of God and rediscover the true protocol of His kingdom? My prayer is that you will heed the words of your heavenly Father while you still have time.

Awake, all nations! Hear the voice of your King.

2

Seek First the Kingdom

ONE OF THE first things we must learn regarding the nature of the kingdom of God is that the principles of kingdom authority that God has set in place cannot be altered or ignored. He says, "Seek ye first. . . ." That commandment is foundational to everything else. Why? Because when we seek Him first, everything else falls into place. Accordingly, we naturally discover God's righteousness.

That's why David could declare, "I have been young, and now am old; yet I have not seen the righteous forsaken, nor his descendants begging bread" (Ps. 37:25). *Righteousness* is a very special word that can only be used in reference to the kingdom of God. Oh, you may be able to come up with some persuasive examples of good behavior and decency in other places, but you won't find genuine righteousness anywhere else but the kingdom of God.

God's kingdom is not the only kingdom around. There are at least two others, and they're both at war with the kingdom of God. God's kingdom was established before the others. It is perfect and eternal. But the other kingdoms were conceived in wickedness and established in rebellion.

The kingdom established by God is the kingdom of heaven. At one time Lucifer was part of it. We know that Lucifer served the Lord at one time, but he forgot that there could be only one Person on the throne; he felt that he should share power with his Maker. It wasn't

15

simply what he said or did; it was what he thought in his imagination that brought Lucifer to ruin!

Lucifer, who became Satan, was created by God and had a relationship with Him. He was an angel of light. So far as we know, he was fully submitted to God until one day when he suddenly saw the throne in a different light; he imagined in his heart that he could sit upon that throne. At that moment he decided he would go against God's authority. But what did God do? Was He tolerant of Satan's rights? Did they have a little talk about diversity and sensitivity training? Absolutely not! God kicked him out the door.

Lucifer, the angel of light, who had been in the very presence of God, fell like lightning from the sky because he thought he could assume God's authority and create a kingdom of his own in the minds of men. Ultimately, it would be a failed attempt, of course. Everything he touched from that day on would turn to ashes. But Satan came to earth with the idea of claiming everything here for himself and destroying whatever he could not possess. He would defile the Garden of Eden and sow seeds of discontent among the sons of men, destroying the peace and harmony of the world God had created.

The reason God wants to be first in our lives is not simply because He enjoys being "Numero Uno." In fact, from a human perspective, I sometimes think that God really has a terrible job. Imagine, to be Lord of so many subjects who are so terribly ungrateful so much of the time! But God's Word is law. All our ideas about law and order are to be based on His authority; there can be no greater authority than that. That's why God established His standard of order among leaders at every level of our spiritual and temporal lives.

Paul says, "He Himself gave some to be apostles, some prophets, some evangelists, and some pastors and teachers, for the equipping of the saints for the work of ministry, for the edifying of the body of Christ" (Eph. 4:11–12). God, the Giver of the law and the ultimate Authority, desires that we understand and follow His plan for order and balance in this world.

Our idea of leadership is not some accident of history. It's not some unique cultural phenomenon. And don't think we can blame it on some ancient patriarchal system, as the feminists do. The Bible's teaching on order and authority is important because it is God's plan. It's His idea of order. That's why we must obey.

He desires, for example, that we acknowledge His view of leadership in the home. We have many broken homes today, but God's model tells us that there cannot be a family without a father and a mother. There should be a father at the head of every household. If the father is not there, for whatever reason, then the mother must become the leader in the home. Without godly leadership and direction, judgment is inevitable to come upon that house. It's not accidental or arbitrary. It's not some modern social phenomenon. God made it that way.

The world's system is not the one established by God. Instead, Satan transported his arrogance and defiance onto the world's stage. The system that dominates modern culture is an order that antagonizes the kingdom of God.

This world's notion of order is actually the culmination of Satan's scheme. Men have "exchanged the truth of God for the lie, and worshiped and served the creature rather than the Creator" (Rom. 1:25). That is a reality we face each day. But the only world God will ever sanction is the kingdom ruled by the Son of His love—our Lord and Savior Jesus Christ. That's the kingdom we must seek, not the kingdom of darkness.

Let me say something here: God will have the last word in this debate. Lucifer's kingdom is already suffering from terminal illness, and his days are numbered. He will not last forever. Nor will the people he rules today. He will not always have control over the minds of men as he does at this moment. People need to be reminded that they don't have to submit to the devil. The people Satan has kept in captivity all these years will either be set free by God or destroyed by Satan. "Therefore submit to God," says the apostle James. "Resist the devil and he will flee from you" (James 4:7).

SEEING WITH NEW EYES

WHEN SATAN WAS thrown out of the kingdom of light, he inherited a world of darkness. Darkness, which is sin, is the opposite of light; Satan's idea of order is the opposite of God's righteousness. Some of

I Have Seen the Kingdom

us know about that; we once lived in darkness. Paul says:

> Do you not know that the unrighteous will not inherit the
> kingdom of God? Do not be deceived. Neither fornicators,
> nor idolaters, nor adulterers, nor homosexuals, nor sodomites,
> nor thieves, nor covetous, nor drunkards, nor revilers, nor
> extortioners will inherit the kingdom of God.
> —1 CORINTHIANS 6:9–10

Why would Paul make such a strong statement? Because we
need to know that the kingdom of darkness can have no connection with the kingdom of light. And then he continues, "And such
were some of you" (v. 11).

Some of us were once captives in the land of the dead, in the
kingdom of darkness where we could not perceive the things of
God. We could not see the light. We did not understand it. We had
no understanding of those who lived in the light. When the world
looks at believers today, they say, "Who are those strange people?
What is all that hocus-pocus they're speaking? Why are they so
high and mighty, talking about their religion all the time?" Those
who inhabit the kingdom of darkness cannot comprehend the light
because their deeds are evil (John 3:19–20).

Have you ever wondered why the Christian faith seems so
strange to those who live by the world's values? It's very simple.
Those who live in darkness are blinded by light when it confronts
them. Those who come out of the darkness into the light have to
refocus their eyes. They have to learn a new way of seeing.

The enemy operates in the dark. If we don't see him, or if we
think we can live as if he is not there, then the deceiver is free to
operate with subtle and cunning power. Those held captive in
Satan's kingdom live in darkness. Since they are unable to see the
light of God's truth, they throw stones at those who dare to walk
according to Christ's commands. Those who are in the light cannot
see into the darkness with their natural eyes, so we have to depend
on the Holy Spirit to provide a supernatural shield.

That's where many believers get into trouble. They don't have
eyes to see Satan's wiles—their spiritual eyes aren't well-developed.

They may not realize that God has provided a shield to protect them from Satan's power. Those who live in the light will always be targets of the enemy, but we don't have to be defeated by him. The Holy Spirit gives us a shield so the enemy's stones will bounce off. As citizens of the kingdom, we have access to supernatural strength. We have been given powerful weapons of faith to defend ourselves, but we have to know that they're there before we can take advantage of them.

Satan hates those who walk in the light with a passion. At one time he held a privileged position. He lived in the light, but greed, pride, and jealousy filled his heart, and he lost his status. He is in darkness today, but he won't be there for long. God has other plans for him. The very chains that Satan has used to bind men and women through the centuries will be used to chain and bind the archdeceiver in the bottomless pit. I like what the Book of Revelation says:

> Then the seventh angel sounded: And there were loud voices in heaven, saying, "The kingdoms of this world have become the kingdoms of our Lord and of His Christ, and He shall reign forever and ever!"
>
> —REVELATION 11:15

The good news is not only that Jesus is already reigning in this kingdom, but that you and I, and all who believe upon His name, will be called upon to reign with Him at that time.

Isn't that an exciting thought? We will reign with Christ. But before we can rule, we must be filled with the light of His truth. We must be equipped as agents of God's authority. The only way anyone can reign in any kingdom is to be an heir to the throne. So Christ is working among us today, in this kingdom, to renew our minds and prepare us to reign with Him in His eternal kingdom. He wants to make us joint heirs with Himself.

Jesus Christ is the Lord of light. He brought His divine love into the world to dispel the darkness from our souls. We were once bound by the enemy. We were once in chains. We were deprived of the life of God and the bread of Christ. But, praise God, Christ came and gave His life on the cross to set us free. In fact, when you

19

begin to see all these things in that light, you finally begin to appreciate what the shed blood of Christ really means.

The blood of Jesus did not just wash us clean. It poured life into our spiritual veins so that our hearts could be made right with God. The Holy Spirit has taken up residence within us so that the blood of Christ can wash away all the impurities, pride, and decay of this world. When Christ becomes the Lord, we receive a miraculous transfusion. His righteousness replaces Satan's lies, and we can be filled with the light of God's truth. Children of the King, washed in the blood of the Lamb, have received a Holy Ghost transfusion!

Jesus says, "I am the light of the world. He who follows Me shall not walk in darkness, but have the light of life" (John 8:12). He says, "Let Me transfuse My life in you, because you cannot rule in My kingdom unless you have the royal blood." So the cleansing blood of Christ enters every aspect of our lives—conscious and subconscious. It flows through every vein and purifies us so that when we stand before God, He sees Christ in us. And the enemy too sees that Christ's blood has been applied to our hearts.

THE HIGH PRICE OF SALVATION

THE BLOOD OF Jesus and the indwelling presence of the Holy Spirit have come to make us new from within. We have been transformed by the renewing of our minds and filled with the Holy Spirit of God. Our minds and spirits have been infused with the blood of Jesus. We are cleansed. This blood is not just a physical thing; it's also a spiritual thing. Can't you hear the words of that old song?

> What can wash away my sin?
> Nothing but the blood of Jesus.
> What can make me whole again?
> Nothing but the blood of Jesus.
>
> Oh! precious is the flow
> That makes me white as snow;
> No other fount I know,
> Nothing but the blood of Jesus!

Too often today's believers don't want to talk about the blood of Jesus. It's too morbid for us. Too messy, we say. But if we really understood the high price that Jesus Christ paid for our salvation, and if we really knew what a treasure His shed blood bestows upon those who are covered by its flow, we would talk about little else! Anyone who has lived in a kingdom where people have shed their blood to give their sovereign the right to rule and to reign will surely understand what the shed blood signifies.

Most of us have no idea what the kingdom is all about. Our understanding of it is so limited, and the images we have are mostly wrong. We have an image in our minds of a regal establishment "Made in the USA." But the kingdom of God existed in heaven eternally, with royal dimensions beyond anything the mind of man can conceive. It is a vast, majestic realm, grander than anything in human history. It is the very kingdom of God.

The Bible says, "Eye has not seen, nor ear heard, nor have entered into the heart of man the things which God has prepared for those who love Him" (1 Cor. 2:9). We cannot imagine the grandeur that has been prepared for us in Christ's eternal kingdom. But we can be secure in the knowledge that His kingdom will be spectacular beyond imagination. So, today, we need to focus our minds on living in the kingdom that is "among us" here and now. Matthew's Gospel admonishes us:

> Therefore I say to you, do not worry about your life, what you will eat or what you will drink; nor about your body, what you will put on. Is not life more than food and the body more than clothing? Look at the birds of the air, for they neither sow nor reap nor gather into barns; yet your heavenly Father feeds them. Are you not of more value than they?
> —MATTHEW 6:25–26

Do you understand what Jesus is saying in these words? Not only is He telling us not to worry about the details of our daily lives, but He is saying that we are not even to worry about what we need to sustain life. Yes, some things are more important than others. But we are not supposed to be overly concerned about this life. We're not to worry about what we eat or drink or wear. Isn't life more important than food? Isn't the body more important than the clothes we wear? Jesus goes on to say:

> Which of you by worrying can add one cubit to his stature? So why do you worry about clothing? Consider the lilies of the field, how they grow: they neither toil nor spin; and yet I say to you that even Solomon in all his glory was not arrayed like one of these. Now if God so clothes the grass of the field, which today is, and tomorrow is thrown into the oven, will He not much more clothe you, O you of little faith?
>
> Therefore, do not worry, saying, "What shall we eat?" or "What shall we drink?" or "What shall we wear?" For after all these things the Gentiles seek. For your heavenly Father knows that you need all these things. But *seek first the kingdom of God and His righteousness*, and all these things shall be added to you.
>
> —MATTHEW 6:27–33, EMPHASIS ADDED

In those powerful last words of verse 33, Jesus emphasizes what He has just said. Seek *first,* before everything else, the kingdom of heaven—that is, the kingdom of God and His righteousness—and all the other things you will need in your life will be provided.

The Lord does not say that we should take care of our jobs first and then think about the things of God second. He doesn't allow us to make His kingdom a part-time job. He doesn't tell us to bow our heads and give Him a little "thank You" when we get that new promotion or raise or whenever something good happens. He doesn't say to go ahead and pay our bills first and then give God what's left over. He says very clearly: "Seek *first* the kingdom of God!"

These are not my words; they're the words of God. They mean that we are not supposed to squeeze Him into our schedules. Our schedules are *not* more important than God. He is more important than any schedule we will ever have. He knows that whatever takes preeminence in our lives will be the thing we worship, and He tells us that He must come first—always.

We are to worship Him and no other. He assures us that if we

22

seek Him *first,* then everything we need to live life to the fullest *shall* be added unto us. Please notice the definite future tense: Everything we need *shall be* added.

KINGDOM MATH

IF WE ARE constantly struggling with subtractions and divisions in our lives, maybe it's because we haven't been giving God first priority. Are God and His kingdom the second or third priority? That kind of math doesn't compute in the kingdom. Christ makes it very clear that if we put His kingdom second, we will not benefit from the riches of our inheritance, but from whatever kingdom we've given preeminence. That other kingdom will have to provide all the things we need.

If we give our attention to something other than what the Father has ordained, we cannot be guaranteed God's undivided attention. We'll soon discover that God has no interest in things from any kingdom but His own. In kingdom math, nothing can be added to God's creation. His kingdom is more important than anything we can come up with on our own. That's why God doesn't hear the prayers of those outside the kingdom. He knows that all the things they've been chasing are just temporary illusions.

How often do we pray these words? "For Thine is the kingdom, the power, and the glory forever." Those words should have real meaning in our lives—they should not be just some rote expression memorized sometime in the past. God wants us to concentrate on the kingdom, and He wants us to learn about His power and His glory.

Satan's kingdom is temporary. Soon it will be a thing of the past. God will confiscate it and take back what belongs to Him. Those who love Jesus are going to reign with Him throughout eternity. If we are children of the King, we are going to rule, but there is something we need to know. We have no right to rule and reign unless the King has invited us to share His throne.

The King is the one who judges. God committed all judgment to His Son. Jesus can do the job alone—He doesn't need our help. But, of His own free will, He has chosen to prepare us to reign with

Him and to judge the earth with Him. "I will not do it alone," He says. "There are others whom I have chosen as kings and priests to reign with Me, to rule with Me, and to judge the world with Me."

We didn't sign up for it. It's not our right. You and I don't know how to rule and reign with Christ! But God has prepared and equipped us to sit on the throne with His Son, and He is preparing us even now for that task. Therefore, one day you and I are going to judge the world. Can you believe it? One day we are going to judge the world!

Paul says, "Let this mind be in you, which was also in Christ Jesus" (Phil. 2:5, KJV). We are to imitate Christ, live by His model, come after Him, take up our cross daily, and follow Him. That's how we learn to rule and reign. If we have the mind of Christ in us, then He can teach us. But we can have the mind of Christ only if we have been invited into the King's chamber. That's where the sheep are separated from the goats, to use the Lord's own expression from Matthew 25.

There is a reason why the kingdom of God is not very popular in modern society. It's because even the children of God don't really understand the rules of the kingdom. I don't say this to belittle any person or group, but 80 percent of preachers today have no clear understanding of the kingdom of God. Why do I say that? Because we can only think in terms of the societies we know, and most of our Western societies are republics—they're not kingdoms.

We cannot grasp the concept of someone staying on the throne forever. In our world, leaders are elected to office. They go in and out of power, in and out of fashion, in and out of favor. If we don't like the way they conduct themselves in office, we can impeach them or toss them out.

America is built on the principle of a republic. A republic is a government of the people, by the people, and for the people. But that's not the way it works in the kingdom. The kingdom of God is a theocracy. A theocracy is a government designed and run entirely by God—and that makes a world of difference.

If we expect to transform the kingdoms of this world into the kingdom of heaven through our own efforts, we're doomed before we begin. The kingdoms of this world will never become the kingdom of our Lord until Christ Himself comes to rule and to reign. (See Revelation 11:15.)

We've got to choose between these two kingdoms. Either we will belong to the kingdom of this world and give ourselves over to the seduction of sin, or we'll belong to the kingdom of Christ. Christians are often unwilling to do the hard, demanding, and demeaning work that has to be done to establish God's kingdom. We want it the easy way. We don't really want spiritual rewards—we want houses, cars, money, success—not that God is against these things, He wants us to have them—but the priority we place upon these things is at issue. How can we expect to overcome Satan's legions and reclaim the nation for Christ if we capitulate to the values of today's world system?

God allows society to be governed by earthly leaders who have the authority to rule. Whether we like them or not, we are responsible to pray for them. We're not called to bash or slander them; we're called to bless them. Unless the secular authority attempts to coerce our beliefs or compel us to violate God's laws, we are expected to obey the law of the land.

The Bible teaches that we are to bless our persecutors. Jesus said:

> Love your enemies, bless them that curse you, do good to them that hate you, and pray for them which despitefully use you, and persecute you; that ye may be the children of your Father which is in heaven: for he maketh his sun to rise on the evil and on the good, and sendeth rain on the just and on the unjust.
>
> —MATTHEW 5:44–45, KJV

Our job, then, is to respect those whom God has empowered for the governing of our nations.

To Set the Captives Free

WHEN TALKING ABOUT the kingdom of God, we need to know that almost every kingdom is established by war. God kicked the devil out of heaven. Remember? He said to Michael, the archangel, "Michael, get rid of this thing!" And Michael got rid of the devil.

I Have Seen the Kingdom

(See Revelation 12:7–9.) God has assured us that His kingdom will never again be interrupted. Even though Satan's insurrection led to the downfall of a third of the angels in heaven and created an adversary kingdom, God has made it perfectly clear that His kingdom will continue forever. When the angel Gabriel appeared to Mary, he clearly stated that God's kingdom would never end:

> And behold, you will conceive in your womb and bring forth a Son, and shall call His name JESUS. He will be great, and will be called the Son of the Highest; and the Lord God will give Him the throne of His father David. And He will reign over the house of Jacob forever, and of His kingdom there will be no end.
>
> —LUKE 1:31–33

Do you hear that? His kingdom shall have no end, and no one will ever successfully challenge His authority. If we don't understand the kingdom of God and use only logic and common sense, we might conclude that we can democratize God. Some of us try to make God into a Republican or a Democrat instead of the autocrat of the entire world. Some of our churches try to do it, too. They elect a pastor, yet the minute he says something controversial or unpopular, they vote him out. They use democracy to try to administer a kingdom that is, by nature, a theocracy.

In a democracy you can speak your mind. Moreover, a child can put his parents in jail if he can come up with a compelling enough argument for the court of public opinion. In a democracy a child can insult you whenever he feels like it, but you cannot administer a spanking, no matter how badly he may need it, for risk of offending the powers that be. If you touch a child in a democratic state today you go straight to jail. But in a theocracy, there is immutable law and order and discipline.

What happens when people try to interpret God's laws with democratic principles? It simply doesn't work. In a democracy, you can go wherever you like because it's a free society. You can speak whenever you feel like it, do whatever you feel like doing, or insult anybody you choose. But don't try that in a theocracy, and don't try it in the kingdom of God. A different standard reigns in God's kingdom. Because most of us have been taught only the concept of a democracy, we have strained relationships with God.

When John the Baptist came into Judea, he preached the kingdom of God and called the people to repentance. That was his job. Why was he doing that? Because at one time we were all part of the kingdom. But when Satan fell, his sin affected everyone born into this world. First he tempted Eve and convinced her to sin against God; from that moment on, every one of us has been born in sin. We are natural-born rebels. John's message called for people to "repent and be baptized." Why? "For the kingdom of heaven is at hand."

John was anointed, inspired, and fearless. Jesus said that this wild-eyed man of God who lived in the desert and fed on locusts and wild honey was the greatest of all the prophets: "Among those born of women there has not risen one greater than John the Baptist" (Matt. 11:11). But He also said something very remarkable: "He who is least in the kingdom of heaven is greater than [John]." What a great honor, but what a great challenge!

Repentance means "turning around and going in a new direction," a complete change of heart and mind. We can't keep going in the same direction. We have to repent and get back to where we're supposed to be. The kingdom has come, and it is within us. And those who truly understand the kingdom will behave differently than those who don't. The rules are meant to be obeyed in the kingdom.

Most believers today have confessed that Jesus is Lord, but, unfortunately, we don't really understand the word *Lord*. Except for the few hours per week that we're in church, we don't even use the word very often. We're not governed by kings, but by the elected officials we put in office. We give them a few years to prove themselves, and, if we're reasonably satisfied, we put them back for another term or two. But kingdoms are not like that. Kings rule by inheritance and conquest, not election. Traditionally the title *Lord* was reserved for those who proved themselves worthy on the field of battle.

Those who excel in certain fields are occasionally granted the title of lord. The late actor Laurence Olivier was given the title Lord Olivier of Brighton in 1970. The title of lord can only be given by the monarch. To receive such a lofty title, one would have to do something remarkable. The heir of a royal title may be known as lord. Jesus Christ bears this title. Why? Because He did something truly remarkable. He defeated the powers of death and hell.

God said, "Because I am King of all kings, I choose to give Him the title of Lord." God declared through Isaiah, "Behold! My Servant whom I uphold, My Elect One in whom My soul delights! I have put My Spirit upon Him; He will bring forth justice to the Gentiles" (Isa. 42:1). When Jesus was baptized by John in the river Jordan, the Bible says that "the heavens were opened to Him, and He saw the Spirit of God descending like a dove and alighting upon Him. And suddenly a voice came from heaven, saying, 'This is My beloved Son, in whom I am well pleased'" (Matt. 3:16–17). God Himself declared the lordship of His Son.

Kingdoms in Conflict

Jesus came to preach the Good News of the kingdom of God. When He began His earthly ministry He shocked the elders by reading aloud in the temple:

> The Spirit of the LORD is upon Me, because He has anointed Me to preach the gospel to the poor; He has sent Me to heal the brokenhearted, to proclaim liberty to the captives and recovery of sight to the blind, to set at liberty those who are oppressed; to proclaim the acceptable year of the LORD.
> —Luke 4:18–19

At that time, the Jews were ruled by governors appointed by Rome. Over the centuries, the children of Israel had been conquered by the Persians, Syrians, Babylonians, Egyptians, and Greeks. They understood what it meant to be dominated by alien powers and to be carried off into slavery.

From the writings of Moses and the prophets we know that the Jews were expecting a Messiah to arise from the people to lead them into the kingdom of God, but, suddenly, here was the son of a simple carpenter declaring His authority to rule the people of God. Obviously, the rulers of the Jews were shocked by His claim.

They knew a thing or two about kings. Ever since the days of Saul and David more than a thousand years earlier, they had been ruled by Hebrew kings; they understood that only a king could appoint a governor. But Jesus stood in the midst of the temple and read the one passage from Isaiah that would make His claim to kingship perfectly clear. So tensions concerning Christ's mission to be proclaimed Messiah and the anointed ruler of the Jews existed from the very beginning of His ministry.

When the Pilgrims first came to these shores in the early seventeenth century, they placed two standards in the sand: the flag of the English king and a Christian cross. From the very beginning, then, the kingdoms of God and man were in competition with each other. The first Americans had learned about kingdoms in England, Holland, and Germany. Over time, however, they modified the system of government to accommodate their vision of freedom and democracy. The Puritans came to establish a nation where they could worship freely, but conflicts between the sacred and the profane existed from the start.

Conflict was inevitable, since no kingdom is ever established without war. Anytime you set out to found a kingdom, there will be war. In the beginning it will be physical warfare, as in the American Revolution. But sooner or later it develops into social, political, intellectual, and spiritual warfare as well. Should we interpret the fact that we are engaged in spiritual battles today to mean that we have failed in the kingdom? Do we think that the conflict between the kingdoms of light and darkness—meaning the kingdoms of God and man—resulted from some kind of cosmic mistake? No. We need to understand that there will always be conflict whenever a kingdom is established.

We can easily get ourselves into trouble if we don't understand the way kingdoms work. And we will never be able to resist the kingdom of darkness if we have a democratic mind-set. We need to understand that we're not fighting against flesh and blood, but against spiritual wickedness in heavenly places. We are dealing with spiritual warfare beyond the human dimension, and we must rely on spiritual weapons in order to fight offensively and at the same time defend ourselves against the kingdom of darkness.

This was the principle Jesus was advocating when He asked Peter and the disciples, "Who do men say that I, the Son of Man, am?" He knew very well what the Pharisees and the Sadducees had been saying about Him. They were part of the conspiracy to prevent Him from succeeding as the spiritual leader of His people. They had conspired to set up kingdoms of their own. In answer to His question, Peter said, "Some say John the Baptist, some Elijah, and others Jeremiah or one of the prophets." Jesus said, "But who do you say that I am?" (Matt. 16:13–16).

This was the testimony for which He had been waiting. In a sense, all creation awaited the same, for by his declaration Peter recognized Jesus as the legitimate ruler of the kingdom of heaven. Peter said, "You are the Christ, the Son of the living God." Peter had never before gone quite so far in his own logic. But there was another surprise yet to come. Yes, he saw Jesus as his Master, his Teacher, and a Shepherd of the people. But until this moment, he had never voiced such words, because God had not yet led him to do so.

When Peter made his important declaration—which may have surprised even himself—Jesus said, "Blessed are you, Simon Bar-Jonah, for flesh and blood has not revealed this to you, but My Father who is in heaven" (v. 17). Then what does it say in the following verses? Jesus says, "I tell you the truth, Peter, I will build My church on this declaration, and the gates of Hell—the legitimate domain of Satan and his demons—will not be able to overcome My plan." Jesus said that when He completed His mission, He would ascend to the Father to prepare a place for us, and He would present the keys of the kingdom to everyone who believes on His name.

What follows is very important, for Jesus then says, "Whatever you bind on earth will be bound in heaven, and whatever you loose on earth will be loosed in heaven" (v. 19). In other words, those who man the kingdom will not be left powerless after His Ascension. They would have kingdom power—miraculous power and gifts of the Spirit to perform all the mighty works that Jesus Himself had done. But He warned the disciples not to tell anyone what had happened. For no one can enter the kingdom of heaven by hearsay. Each must find his or her own way into the kingdom by genuine faith in the Son of God.

Here again, Jesus reveals the nature of the kingdom. Later, He tells them that when the Son of man comes in His glory with legions of angels, and He sits on His throne, all the nations will be gathered before Him. He will separate the people one from another. He will put the righteous on one side and the wicked on the other. To the righteous He will say, "Come, you who are blessed of My Father, accept the inheritance that was prepared for you before the creation of the world. Take it, it's yours!" What is your inheritance? The kingdom that God the Father prepared for you before the foundations of the earth.

When Jesus Christ finishes His work, He will take His throne. Today He sits at the right hand of God the Father, interceding for us. He is our spokesman, our ambassador, our mediator. He has given us His Holy Spirit to defend us, to teach us, to school our hearts and minds in the rules of the kingdom, while He sits at the right hand of God. What does it mean to sit at the right hand of God? It means that Christ has the authority to speak for His Father in the kingdom.

Jesus says, "If you hear what I am saying, then you have heard My Father. If you believe in Me, then you are believing in Him as well." That's what it means. Jesus is at the right hand of God, and He speaks with all the authority and majesty of God the Father.

Governments come and go, but the kingdom of God remains forever. Democracies come and go, but God's kingdom is secure. The principles of the kingdom that we are learning in these pages are principles the whole world needs to know. They can learn them from us if we are prepared to teach them. Others can benefit from what we are learning. But we must be willing to tell them.

If we don't do it, someone else will. Christ has given us kingdom authority, and He has given us the Holy Spirit as our Comforter and Guide. And He has also given us a Great Commission to go into all the world and make disciples. Are you willing to do that? When Jesus taught the disciples about what would happen in the End Times, He said, "This gospel of the kingdom will be preached in all the world as a witness to all the nations, and then the end will come" (Matt. 24:14). Jesus' intention was not only to make disciples, but to teach them to observe His kingdom principles (Matt. 28:19–20). So the truth of the kingdom will be proclaimed to the ends of the earth. Are you doing your part to spread the kingdom of God?

You're a Child of the King

IF YOU DON'T understand what I have been saying so far, then the principles of the kingdom will not make sense to you. Jesus says that the gospel of His kingdom must be preached to the whole world so that every person on this planet will have access to God's plan of Redemption. When the end comes, Christ will judge the nations by the standards of the kingdom.

No one gets citizenship in the kingdom by accident. It's relatively easy to become a citizen of a country here on earth. If you apply for citizenship, live right, do the right things, and have spent a long time living in a country, you can become a citizen. You may not speak the language very well at first, but you can become a citizen if you learn the culture, fill out the necessary paperwork, and do what's expected of a citizen.

In the closing verses of the Book of Revelation we find this fascinating image.

> And the Spirit and the bride say, "Come!" And let him who hears say, "Come!" And let him who thirsts come. Whoever desires, let him take the water of life freely.
> —REVELATION 22:17

Jesus has said that anyone who will take up his cross and follow Him can become part of the kingdom of God and receive citizenship in the eternal city. But here we see that it is the Holy Spirit and the bride of Christ, which is the worldwide Christian church, who call out to the lost, saying, "Come to Christ! Come and receive the water of life!" Brothers and sisters, that means you and I have the keys to the kingdom. We have the power and the authority, as heirs of the kingdom, to invite others to receive the gift of eternal life.

Are we doing that? Are we faithful to this important task that Jesus has given us? We have been made sons and fellow heirs of the kingdom. Paul says, "And because you are sons, God has sent forth the Spirit of His Son into your hearts." If we are truly sons and heirs, then no man can make us his slave. We are no longer in bondage to sin, lust, and pride, but we have a new identity in the kingdom of God. Paul continues, "Therefore you are no longer a slave but a son, and if a son, then an heir of God through Christ" (Gal. 4:6–7).

When you are the child of the king, you must learn how to conduct yourself as a son or daughter of nobility. Ministers will teach you proper manners and how to conduct yourself with dignity. Unfortunately, some of us aren't good pupils. We do whatever we want to do. A king's kid never eats junk—the king wants a healthy heir. A king's kid cannot sleep just anywhere he chooses—he is to be protected by the palace guards at all times. That's where safety lies, and the king wants his heir to be safe.

Some of us are King's kids, but we've been devoting our energies in the wrong places. King's kids are trained as to how to conduct themselves. (See Galatians 4:1–2.) They're taught how to walk, talk, sit, stand, and eat properly. They don't have to go to bed hungry, and they're not to be mistreated in any way. If the child of a king is mistreated, the world will say, "So this is how the king treats his children!" Isn't it a shame how some of us represent our King? Sometimes we behave as if we serve a poor, neglectful, and abusive king!

If earthly kings know how to treat their children, how much more does God know how to treat His sons and daughters? A good king will never withhold any good thing from his sons and daughters. The children of a good king are always protected. His children are not to be subjected to danger. They will be protected. But what would happen if those children were to charge off on their own, doing whatever they wanted to do without the king's permission, living as no child of a king should ever live? Would the king continue to love and support such children? Would he tolerate bad behavior without serious discipline? Not on your life! With much love comes responsibility.

I Have Seen the Kingdom

As children of the King, we have been given an awesome trust. We have been empowered by the greatest King who will ever live to carry the Good News of His kingdom to the uttermost parts of the earth. In return, we have the promise of His eternal love and protection. He will provide for us and see that we have whatever we need, but we must live and conduct ourselves according to the standards of His royal household. Are we doing that today? Are we living with the authority and responsibility of an heir to the kingdom?

I trust that you will find the strength, support, and encouragement in these pages to enable you to live as an heir. I hope what you learn in this and succeeding chapters will give you the motivation to love the Lord your God with all your heart, mind, soul, and strength and to love your neighbors enough to share the Good News of the kingdom with them.

I trust you will take these words to heart and live by them each day: "Seek first the kingdom of God and His righteousness, and all these things shall be added to you" (Matt. 6:33).

3

Life in the Kingdom

WHAT IS KINGDOM LIVING? According to Christ's words to Nicodemus in John 3, the gateway into the kingdom of God is the new birth. Paul tells us that this new life is the evidence of Christ's indwelling Spirit shed abroad in our hearts. He says that if we receive Jesus Christ, then "the love of God has been poured out in our hearts by the Holy Spirit who was given to us" (Rom. 5:5). When we become citizens of the kingdom, we walk and talk with God, and His Spirit lives within us. That is the essence of kingdom living.

In Matthew 4:23 we see that Jesus went all about the province of Galilee preaching and teaching the gospel of the kingdom. So we have already received the kingdom of God in our hearts, but that's far different from the stories we've heard about some far-off kingdom in the sky. We sing songs like, "In the sweet by and by, we shall meet on the beautiful shore. . . . " We talk about the kingdom as if it were some fanciful vision or some fairy-tale world of imagination up in the sky. But that's far from the truth.

If you are a believer and living by the Word of God, you are already living in the kingdom of God. We have all been given the opportunity to operate in the kingdom. But most of us need some operating instructions. Unless we know how to operate successfully in the kingdom here and now, we won't know how to function in the celestial kingdom when we get there. If we don't know how to live victoriously in this life, we can hardly be expected to be conquerors with Christ when His eternal kingdom is revealed. This life is a training ground, and it is here that we learn how to apply the principles of kingdom living.

The first principle of any kingdom is that somebody has to be in charge. In a true kingdom, there has to be a king. You can't have a kingdom unless you have a king and a royal family that maintains the authority and sets the agenda for the nation. Those who are chosen for positions of leadership in the kingdom bear the authority of the king; they are to carry out his edicts. According to the Word of God, the kingdom of God has been preached to us. We have been translated into the kingdom. We bear the power and authority of the King, and we are therefore authorized to carry out His commands upon this earth.

One of the most remarkable statements of the vital relationship between our heavenly Father and those who dwell in the kingdom is found in John 18, when Jesus is brought before the Roman governor, Pontius Pilate.

> Then Pilate entered the Praetorium again, called Jesus, and said to Him, "Are You the King of the Jews?" Jesus answered him, "Are you speaking for yourself about this, or did others tell you this concerning Me?" Pilate answered, "Am I a Jew? Your own nation and the chief priests have delivered You to me. What have You done?"
>
> Jesus answered, "My kingdom is not of this world. If My kingdom were of this world, My servants would fight, so that I should not be delivered to the Jews; but now My kingdom is not from here." Pilate therefore said to Him, "Are You a king then?"
>
> Jesus answered, "You say rightly that I am a king. For this cause I was born, and for this cause I have come into the world, that I should bear witness to the truth. Everyone who is of the truth hears My voice."
>
> —JOHN 18:33–37

Now remember that in John 14:6 Jesus had already declared the ultimate source of truth. He reassured Thomas, his faithful but doubting disciple, "I am the way, the truth, and the life." Thomas, the intellectual, needed to see to believe, and Jesus gave him all the proof he needed. But since Pilate was a citizen of the Roman Empire and of the secular world—not the kingdom of God—He didn't get it. He didn't understand what Jesus was all about. He didn't grasp His *way* or His *truth*. So we have this remarkable exchange:

> Pilate said to Him, "What is truth?" And when he had said this, he went out again to the Jews, and said to them, "I find no fault in Him at all."
>
> —JOHN 18:38

What is truth? Little did the Roman governor know how important that question truly was. How his words ring out, down through the corridors of time to our own day! How men have agonized over that question, searching in vain for the source of truth!

Pilate was not a Jew. He was a Roman citizen, appointed by the emperor as procurator of Judea. But when Jesus threw his own question back at him, He was saying in essence, "Are you asking this for yourself, Pilate, or did somebody else put you up to it?" In other words, "Whose charges are you bringing, Pilate—your own or those of the Jewish leaders?"

This is an important characteristic of Jesus' teaching method, and He used it often. He knew perfectly well what was going on, but He wanted Pilate to know that He knew. So Pilate had no choice but to answer, "Your own nation and the chief priests have delivered You to me." It was the children of Israel who delivered their Messiah to be judged and, in due course, to be executed by the Romans. We might say that it was a put-up job and that those who had rejected the Good News of the kingdom were behind it all along.

But Jesus says something else very important: "My kingdom is not of this world. If My kingdom were of this world, My servants would fight, so that I should not be delivered to the Jews; but now My kingdom is not from here." While it is true that we have kingdom authority through the power of the Holy Spirit, Jesus says the ultimate and eternal kingdom of God is not here yet. We are told in various places in Scripture that today's world system belongs to Satan. The Bible says, "The earth is the Lord's, and all its fullness" (Ps. 24:1). But the world system that surrounds us is the dominion of the enemy.

A TALE OF TWO KINGDOMS

NO WONDER WE find ourselves in constant conflict. We are caught between two kingdoms! Christ acknowledged our predicament in the high priestly prayer recorded in John 17. Jesus let the disciples know that He was praying for *them,* not for those who are part of this world system. He says that if His disciples were of this world, the world would love them; because they are not of this world, the world will always hate the followers of Christ.

So Jesus prayed, "Father, sanctify them, because they are not of the world." John helped clarify this later when he wrote, "Do not love the world or the things in the world. If anyone loves the world, the love of the Father is not in him" (1 John 2:15).

John also writes, "The world is passing away, and the lust of it; but he who does the will of God abides forever" (1 John 2:17). And in one of the most memorable passages in the entire New Testament, Paul says, "Do not be conformed to this world, but be transformed by the renewing of your mind" (Rom. 12:2). God owns the world, and He has made it fruitful for our benefit. He has allowed men and women to show what they value most.

We have been given the right to choose or reject the Savior by our own free will. And for the time being, it seems the governments and belief systems of this world are securely in the dominion of Satan. The only way we can walk with God, then, is by being transformed and renewed from within.

We see that there are two kingdoms, and we need to know the differences between them. If you're confused about the difference between the *earth* and the *world,* then you're in danger of being misled by the enemy, because Satan knows if you don't know the difference. He knows if you are ignorant about the kingdom of God. That's why Peter counsels us that we should be sober and vigilant, alert to all the wiles of our adversary, the devil. And we need to be able to distinguish how the various terms are used in Scripture.

When Jesus Christ was brought before Pilate, He made it plain that His kingdom was not of this world. If it were of this world, His servants (the heavenly host) would fight for Him. But the principalities and powers of this world (the demons of Satan) are fighting on the other side, waging war against the kingdom of heaven. If we belong to Christ, we share the hope that Paul expresses so eloquently when he says, "For I am persuaded that neither death nor life, nor angels nor principalities nor powers, nor things present nor things to come, nor height nor depth, nor any other created thing, shall be able to separate us from the love of God which is in Christ Jesus our Lord" (Rom. 8:38–39).

When Christ was being arrested, Peter sprang to his Master's defense, grabbing his sword and whacking off the ear of one of the men who had come to arrest Jesus. If the kingdom of heaven were of this world, Jesus might have said, "Yes, that's it, Peter, hit him again! Not just his ear, knock his head off!" But He didn't do that. Instead, He replaced the man's ear and healed him on the spot. Why? Because His servants were not the people standing around Him that night. His servants were angels and ministering spirits from the eternal kingdom. That's why Hebrews 1:14 speaks of "ministering spirits sent forth to minister for those who will inherit salvation."

As we look closely at these remarks, we should perceive that there are, in fact, three kingdoms: the kingdom of God, the kingdom of Satan, and the kingdom of man. Pride took Satan out of the kingdom of God. We are not to walk in the strength of our own knowledge and pride. The Father wants us to be renewed, to be translated from the earthly kingdom, which is the kingdom of Satan, into the kingdom of His Son.

That is why it says in Colossians 1:13 that "He has delivered us from the power of darkness and conveyed us into the kingdom of the Son of His love." The King James Version says He has "translated" us. It's like translating a book from one language into another. God is a God of righteousness, and for Him to be able to read our fallible human lives as righteousness we have to be translated by the blood of Christ. When we bow at the foot of the cross and acknowledge Jesus Christ as our Redeemer and the Lord of our lives, we are translated in that instant from the kingdom of darkness into the kingdom of light.

If you are born again, if Jesus is the Lord of your life, if you believe with your heart unto righteousness, and if you have confessed with your mouth that God has raised Christ from the dead, then you have been ushered into the kingdom of light. Any child of God has the opportunity to live in the kingdom. But a child of God should exhibit kingdom results in his walk of faith. The Bible makes it very plain that "faith without works is dead." In the kingdom of God there must also be works.

We are justified by faith, but our works demonstrate that we are children of the kingdom. We're not saved by works, but we're saved unto good works. Paul says, "For we are his workmanship, created in Christ Jesus unto good works, which God hath before ordained that we should walk in them" (Eph. 2:10, KJV). Remember the story of Rahab in Hebrews 11? The Bible says that Abraham was justified by faith because he had been given a covenant by God, and he believed God would be faithful. But Rahab was not one of the Jewish people; she didn't know what it meant to follow the Law or worship Israel's God. She was justified by her works—by her act of mercy—and that made her part of the household of faith and one of the forebearers of the Messiah.

As believers, we have to understand that there are works in the kingdom. If we are part of the kingdom, God intends for all of us to bear kingdom fruits. We are not to worry about the way to do these things. Any person who thinks and worries constantly is anxious, and the Bible says we are to "be anxious for nothing." Kingdom life demands faith in action.

You don't have to think so; you can know so. If you are operating in the kingdom, you know so by reasoning with God. He has already provided all that you need, but you have the privilege of reasoning with Him. If you're sick, don't think about healing. Reason with God about it. That's where we get into trouble—thinking too much.

If you have marital problems, don't think about how you're going to solve them—reason with God's Word about how to relate to your spouse. If you have financial problems, don't think about how you're going to make more money—reason with God's Word. The answer has already been provided. Christ, through the Spirit of God, does the thinking so we can take it at face value, go ahead, and *just do it.* The Scriptures are our life source.

TRUE PEACE OF MIND

THE BIBLE SAYS, "Be anxious for nothing, but in everything by prayer and supplication, with thanksgiving, let your requests be made known to God; and the peace of God, which surpasses all understanding, will guard your hearts and minds through Christ Jesus" (Phil. 4:6–7). Because we don't worry about what we can do by human strength, but through prayer and supplication make our requests known unto God, guess what happens? The peace of God, which passes all understanding, fills our hearts and minds. We think with our heads, but we reason with our hearts.

If we are operating in the kingdom of God, we will always ask, "What does the Bible say? What does the Word of God tell me to do?" When we operate according to kingdom principles, we bring glory and honor to our King. In the kingdom of God, Christ has been established as Lord of lords and King of kings. When He was riding into Jerusalem to be crucified He rode in dignity, as a king. When He was crucified and overcame death, God highly exalted Him by breaking the power of death and the grave. He ascended to sit at the right hand of God the Father Almighty, with glory and honor.

What Christ is doing right now is reigning. He is our Sovereign, interceding for us. As Paul says, "We live and move and have our being" in the kingdom of Jesus Christ. Have you ever thought about that? Jesus is sitting at the right hand of God. Colossians 3:3 says that our lives are "hidden with Christ in God." Even though we are still on this earth, we are operating in the kingdom. The very moment you were saved, the kingdom of God came to dwell in your heart.

The sovereign rule of God is manifested through the work of Christ within us. It is His purpose to defeat His enemies, to overcome the dominion of Satan in the world, and to create for Himself people of power. Through them He reigns on the earth today. Everyone who voluntarily submits to the rule of Christ is a citizen of the kingdom of God, both here in the physical dimension as well as in the eternal kingdom to come.

We also know that there are aspects of kingdom living that influence and shape every aspect of our lives. In the kingdom of God, for example, there is freedom, salvation, and peace. In the kingdom of God there is new life. The Scriptures tell us in many places that Christ came and established here, among us, all that He saw in the kingdom of God. He said, "The works which the Father has given Me to finish—the very works that I do" (John 5:36). And further, "I speak what I have seen with My Father" (John 8:38).

It's a little bit like when the pastor opens his wedding book at the wedding ceremony and says, "Do you take this woman to be your lawfully wedded wife?"

The groom answers simply, "I do." He doesn't have to go through all the reasons why he chose to get married and all the things he expressed in private to his bride when he proposed to her. He has already assured her of his devotion and confessed his desire to be legally married to her. Now he merely has to affirm, before God and the assembly of family and friends, "I do."

Christ knew before He ever came to earth that He would marry the people of God. He knew, furthermore, that He was going to marry people who were living in sin. But He was going to wash them by His own blood and become the husband and protector of His bride, the church. So when God said to His Son, "Do you choose to go to the earth and die for this people?" Jesus said, "I do." In those words, He committed Himself to provide the Atonement for our sin, which was His own death on the cross, so that He could have lordship over the church.

He knew before the foundation of the world that He was going to do it. When He came, He didn't have to go through all the decisions that had already been made or to restate all the reasons for His decision. He simply said, "I do," and brought the kingdom to this planet. What is the kingdom but the qualities of His devotion—including love, joy, peace, longsuffering, kindness, goodness, faithfulness, gentleness, and self-control—all made perfect through the indwelling presence of the Holy Spirit of God?

When He walked on the earth, He said, "If you want to operate in the kingdom and let people know that you are My disciples, then you must demonstrate your love for one another. Unless you are born again, you really do not know what love is all about." Sadly, there are many people who are born again but who don't know what love is. They are confused. They think love is some emotion. But love is something that goes beyond the natural affections of human beings. Love is a dynamic force that comes only from God.

The Bible says, "God is love, and he who abides in love abides in God, and God in him" (1 John 4:16). Love is a force from the kingdom of God that is revealed by God's divine love toward us. That love was shed abroad in our hearts by Jesus Christ. Anytime He saw the multitudes gathered together to hear His words, He had compassion on them, because He was the visible expression of the kingdom of God on earth. His life demonstrated God's love for all those who are lost.

Anytime believers want to operate in the kingdom of God, then the most basic thing in our lives must be the evidence of that love. First, we must understand what love is all about. We behave more like selfish children many times. God does not operate that way. The driving force in His kingdom is *agape* love. It's like the Energizer bunny—it just keeps going and going and going—without expectation of return.

That's what God did for us. He gave His Son to purchase our eternal life. If we receive Jesus Christ, the love of God is poured out in our hearts. How so? Paul tells us, "The love of God has been poured out in our hearts by the Holy Spirit who was given to us. For when we were still without strength, in due time Christ died for the ungodly" (Rom. 5:5–6). That takes us back to where we started, knowing that "the peace of God, which surpasses all understanding, will guard your hearts and minds through Christ Jesus" (Phil. 4:7).

Isn't that amazing? The peace of God! We have the privilege of walking in the peace that God has ordained for those who know His Son. If you are a Christian man or woman and you have become a citizen of the kingdom, then God wants you to be filled with His peace so that you can operate in the kingdom. I challenge you to ask yourself these questions: "Do I live and move and have my being in that kingdom? Do I rejoice in knowing that I am a child of God, filled with the Holy Spirit, and living each day for Him? Do I cherish that gift of peace? Or am I on another path altogether?"

AN OPEN INVITATION

WILL YOU OPEN your heart to God's love so He can fill you with kingdom love? When Jesus Christ becomes the object and focus of your life, you find that your hopes and aspirations take on a new focus. When your heart is one with the heart of God, you will love others; you will want to reach out to those who do not know Him. Is that how you feel today? Does your heart beat in rhythm with the heart of God? Are you living in the spirit of God's peace? Are you a child of the king?

There are two stages in the kingdom of God: this present kingdom, which is active today in this world, and the future kingdom, which is the ultimate and eternal fulfillment of God's plan for mankind. That is when we will be united with Him for eternity. Jesus said that His ability to cast out demons was evidence that the kingdom of God has come to men. In Matthew 12, we see how Jesus Christ proclaimed His love by setting free those who were in bondage to sin and disease. Then, in John 18:36, we see where Jesus said, "My kingdom is not of this world." In other words, *My kingdom is not part of this world's system.* So there are at least two aspects, or two identities, to the kingdom.

The world has a system that, by and large, is antagonistic to the kingdom of Christ. That is why Christians have been called out of this world. But some might ask, "What about John 3:16?" We all know this wonderful verse, which says, "For God so loved the world that He gave His only begotten Son, that whoever believes in Him should not perish but have everlasting life."

Here is the answer. For God, who made the world and everything in it, loved the work of His hands, including each one of us, so much that He sent His Son to redeem the world from the corruption that evil men, led by their father the devil, brought into the world. He did not say, *For God so loved the system of this world,* but

God loved the people whom the system has held in bondage as slaves. For truly, the sin of this world has made slaves of all those who do not know God. God did not love the material world, but rather, He loved the people to whom He desired to give dominion over it.

Sadly, the men and women He created made the systems of this world, and they are a desperate challenge to God's way of doing things. Our influences and ideas made this world. Our scientists, scholars, philosophers, artists, and thinkers, along with our scientific theories and beliefs, made this world the way it is today. Our carnal and finite sentiments made this world, and it is a world-view of fraud and self-deception that has destroyed the natural beauty of what God had made. It is our social theories, along with the vain musings of those who have held center stage in the affairs of men since the Garden of Eden, that have made the world as it is today. Ultimately, it is our sin that has led to the tragedy, inhumanity, incivility, and despair of our day.

Christ said, "My kingdom is not of this world." To Pilate and to us He says, "My influence does not come as a result of things around Me. My kingdom is from above."

In Ephesians we read, "For we do not wrestle against flesh and blood, but against principalities, against powers, against the rulers of the darkness of this age, against spiritual hosts of wickedness in the heavenly places" (Eph. 6:12). Paul is talking about the forces we fight against every day. We are participants through the Holy Spirit of God in a warfare between the things of God and the things ruled by Satan and his forces.

How do we walk in the kingdom of God? This is what Jesus said: "If My kingdom were of this world, my servants would fight, so that I should not be delivered to the Jews; but now My kingdom is not from here." In other words, He deliberately gave Himself to these Jews to be persecuted, hated, accused, and crucified. But what happened? When He was crucified, a new kingdom began, which was the kingdom of God revealed in the flesh for the redemption of man.

Hear these words of Paul who says, "For the kingdom of God is not eating and drinking, but righteousness and peace and joy in the Holy Spirit" (Rom. 14:17). The world cannot understand the kingdom of God, for it is not something the almighty dollar can provide. It is not made of things that give us life in our natural flesh. Instead, the kingdom of God is righteousness and joy in the Holy Ghost.

You see, joy is a Spirit-thing. We know we are of the kingdom when our hearts are full of joy, because joy, like peace and righteousness, is a product of the Spirit-life. We cannot get righteousness, joy, or peace from this world. Oh, yes, this world promises peace, but it is unable to follow through. It promises us everything we desire, but it fails on every count. The world breaks our hearts, time after time, because its promises are always empty.

I receive the truth of the kingdom only when I receive Jesus Christ into my heart. In fact, the very moment that I receive Jesus into my heart God sets into motion the laws of the kingdom, which are beyond human ability to comprehend. That's why Jesus says the kingdom of God is more than meat and drink.

Paul tells us in Romans 14:17 that the kingdom of Jesus Christ is not something that human beings can lay hands on. Jesus Christ was the ambassador, the chief spokesman, and the heavenly emissary of a kingdom that brings righteousness, joy, and peace in the Holy Ghost, and that is exactly what He brought to us.

Why would Jesus say, "Come to Me, all you who labor and are heavy laden, and I will give you rest" (Matt. 11:28)? Because we want peace, we want joy, and we want righteousness. Our consciences tell us, "You are bad, you've sinned, you are unrighteous, and there's no hope for you." If we are of this world, we accept that. Our minds and bodies tell us that we need freedom. We need peace; we need joy, but we don't know how to get those things. Yet, the very moment that Christ came into our lives, He gave us all of them and so much more.

The kingdom of God is in our midst at this very moment. Jesus Christ is, as Paul said, our down payment on the joys of heaven. He is reigning at this moment in our midst. I like the way the New Living Translation says it: "It is God who gives us, along with you, the ability to stand firm for Christ. He has commissioned us, and he has identified us as his own by placing the Holy Spirit in our hearts as the first installment of everything he will give us" (2 Cor.

1:21–22). Isn't that nice? The moment you receive Christ into your heart, you are plugged into Him.

LIVING WITH AUTHORITY

WHEN THE CURRENT starts to flow, we are filled with the Holy Spirit, and that's when we truly become Christ's body, the church. He is the head, and we are His hands and feet. We are saved by the shed blood of Jesus Christ, our faith in Him, and by confessing Him as Lord. Upon that promise, we are children of the kingdom. Christ says, "Assuredly, I say to you, unless you are converted and become as little children, you will by no means enter the kingdom of heaven" (Matt. 18:3).

Pardon me? A child? That's right. Unless we are converted and become as little children, we shall not enter into the kingdom of God. Maybe I can put it this way: To be a little child of God who is in the kingdom of God you have to be converted. And if you are a child, then you know how a good daddy loves his children. He plays with them. He protects them. God does not expect us to be old men and women in the kingdom. He expects us to be like innocent children, depending on Him for our needs.

He doesn't want us to rely upon our own strength and independence. He wants us to depend on Him, to rely upon Him daily, and to trust Him each day for our needs. Christ prayed, "Give us this day our daily bread." To operate in the kingdom of God we must learn to be reliant upon God's provision. Yet, our human nature teaches us to be self-reliant. We know we should have a mature faith, so we do everything in our own strength, we become selfish, and we're far from living with the faith of children.

"Well, I don't want to be a baby. I mean, I can put on my own tie. I can lace my own shoes! I am not some little boy." Unfortunately, we can't live like that in God's kingdom. We have to be as a child. Unless we are converted and become dependent upon God like a little child, then we will by no means enter the kingdom of heaven.

We have the privilege of coming to the Master as His beloved children. Don't you love Christ's words in the subsequent chapter of Matthew when He says, "Let the little children come to Me, and do not forbid them; for of such is the kingdom of heaven" (Matt. 19:14)? We have been called children of the kingdom because we have been converted.

He says, "Do not forbid the little children to come unto Me; they are a perfect illustration of what the kingdom of heaven will be like." They are tender, hopeful, gentle, and enthusiastic, with all the qualities of innocence that Christ desires each of us to possess. That's why He calls for us to become children of the kingdom.

There's a paradox in this, however, and it is very important that we recognize it at this point. As I have said, God expects us to enter His kingdom as children. The Scripture makes that very clear, but He also expects us, once we are citizens of the kingdom, to be able to use our kingdom authority.

What does that mean? How is it possible to be innocent, meek, and tender, like children, and then to have dominion over the earth and wield power over principalities, powers, the rulers of the darkness of this age, and over spiritual hosts of wickedness in the heavenly places? How can those two things exist together? The answer is simple: It's a divine paradox, and it can only happen in the kingdom of God.

This is an area that a large proportion of the evangelical church today does not fully understand. This is where many in the so-called mainstream churches get themselves into trouble, and it's why they seldom, if ever, take advantage of the healing power that God has given His children. They walk down the aisle, get their citizenship papers, and then proclaim, "Praise God, brother, I'm saved!" And that's it. It's over!

After the first blush of excitement, they go back to living pretty much as they've always lived. They don't tell anybody they're living in the kingdom of God. Their pastors and teachers fail to teach them the truths of kingdom authority. They behave like good little children, but they never take hold of the other part. They never lay claim to the power that belongs to every child of the kingdom. When they get sick, instead of casting out sickness and disease, they spiritualize their illness. "Oh, praise God, I'm sick. Now watch me, brother, and see how I suffer for the Lord!"

Do they really think that God wants them to be sick? They must, since they spend so much time learning all kinds of spiritual lessons about suffering, holiness, and being brokenhearted. They allow Satan to deprive them of the power that God wants His children to possess. "Oh, God brought this burden on me," they moan, as if kingdom life is all about suffering and illness.

Instead of learning how to use their authority, too often they quote Scriptures: "Oh, God sent some angels to disturb Paul, so if Paul was able to bear it, then I'll just bear it, too." Such ignorance fills the kingdom of God. This attitude of holy resignation, I believe, is the result of wrong teaching.

How can we talk about a person being born again, entering into eternal life with the Father, and beginning to learn about life in His kingdom, but then fail to see that our Father expects us to live the kingdom life and to enjoy what He has provided for us here? Listen, my dear friend, your heavenly Father loves you! He has not put you out here in the wilderness to survive on your own! He has put awesome resources in your hands—the very treasures of heaven are at your disposal. But if you want to live as God meant for you to live, then you're going to have to learn how to operate in the kingdom of God!

In Deuteronomy 8:18 God spoke to the people just after He had given them the Ten Commandments, teaching them how they should live in the land He had given them. He said, "And you shall remember the LORD your God, for it is He who gives you power to get wealth, that He may establish His covenant which He swore to your fathers, as it is this day." That is a kingdom truth. God gives the power to get wealth to every child of the kingdom. But unless we know the principles of the kingdom and operate in the kingdom, then we can never use the power He has freely given us.

The wealth described here does not mean winning the lottery! It is not accumulated by ripping people off in some land scam! God is not promising that you're going to come into some giant windfall if you play your cards right. But He is saying that He has given us a good and abundant land, He has blessed us richly, and if we use our talents wisely and seek God's will in everything we do, then we will prosper, flourish, and fill the land with the dividends of our labor.

I Have Seen the Kingdom

You will not go broke; you will live prosperously.

Remember what we saw in Romans 14:17? Paul says, "The kingdom of God is not eating and drinking, but righteousness and peace and joy in the Holy Spirit." Like David in Psalm 51, we desire that God will restore to us the joy of our salvation, but unless we know that there is righteousness, joy, and peace through the Holy Spirit in the kingdom of God, we will never enjoy it. So we have to go beyond what we know and feel to grasp what God is offering us.

OVERCOMING THE EVIL ONE

IF WE HAVE come to Jesus Christ by opening our hearts to Him, then He wants us to know that the kingdom of God belongs to us. It belongs to you, but you have to learn how to talk the kingdom talk, walk the kingdom walk, sleep the kingdom sleep, jump the kingdom jump, and run the kingdom race. Many people who get saved have a head knowledge of salvation, but their souls are absent from the kingdom. That is exactly what Satan wants. If he can get you to withhold your heart from the kingdom of God, then he gets you in the bargain, and that's just what he wants.

Satan wants to work on the things around you and take your mind off the kingdom of God to keep you from applying the principles of God's kingdom. Anytime you obey the devil rather than God, you are deprived of peace, joy, and righteousness in the Holy Spirit. Instead of rejoicing in God's provision, you walk around consumed by your guilt, failure, disappointment, and hurt. That always happens anytime you concede to Satan's lies rather than sticking to the truth of God's Word.

Jesus taught that the kingdom of God is like a small amount of leaven put into a lump of flour—that little bit of yeast will eventually transform the whole lump. Now that doesn't mean that the kingdom of God is something that ferments, but rather that the kingdom spreads. It is like a grain of mustard that is so small you can hardly see it in the palm of your hand, but when it's properly planted and nourished, it grows until it is a huge healthy plant that reproduces itself and covers the earth. So the kingdom of God produces fruit after its kind. Christ came to represent the kingdom of God for us.

If Christ operated in the power of the kingdom, preached the gospel of the kingdom, and healed the sick, then obviously He wants believers to do the same. He wants us to operate in the gifts of the Spirit. He wants us to talk the way He talked. When He sent out the seventy evangelists in Luke 10, He commissioned them to go out and teach whatever He had taught them, to speak as He had spoken, and to perform the same signs and wonders that He had done. "He who hears you hears Me," He said. "He who rejects you rejects Me, and he who rejects Me rejects Him who sent Me" (v. 16).

The seventy followed Christ's orders when they went out. They preached, healed, and taught the gospel of the kingdom; they were overjoyed at the results. Luke says:

> Then the seventy returned with joy, saying, "Lord, even the demons are subject to us in Your name." And He said to them, "I saw Satan fall like lightning from heaven. Behold, I give you the authority to trample on serpents and scorpions, and over all the power of the enemy, and nothing shall by any means hurt you. Nevertheless do not rejoice in this, that the spirits are subject to you, but rather rejoice because your names are written in heaven."
>
> —LUKE 10:17–20

Again, here is evidence of the authority of those who inhabit the kingdom. Christ who had all power, who witnessed Lucifer's fall from heaven like lightning from the sky, has entrusted His own kingdom authority into our hands. Isn't that a tremendous risk for Him to take? Yes, it is, because we do fail from time to time. There are times when we misuse our trust. But Jesus assures us that He loves us, He trusts us, and He knows that, one way or the other, He will glorify the kingdom of God through us if we continue to live as we have been taught through His Word.

The Bible says that we must heed these lessons so that we may grow. This is the only way we can hope to overcome the wicked one. Unless we learn how to live and to walk in the kingdom, we cannot accomplish all that Christ has planned for us. How many churches really practice kingdom living today? We talk about the love of God, but do we really demonstrate the kind of *agape* love that Christ demonstrated in His earthly ministry?

We talk about believing the whole Word of God, but we ignore the parts that are hard to understand or that conflict with our notions about propriety, decorum, and modern science. We don't want to risk using our kingdom authority, just in case it doesn't work. We don't want to be embarrassed. Isn't that right? But the Bible says, "Is anyone among you sick? Let him call for the elders of the church, and let them pray over him, anointing him with oil in the name of the Lord. And the prayer of faith will save the sick, and the Lord will raise him up. And if he has committed sins, he will be forgiven" (James 5:14–15). Now that is an awesome testimony from a man who should know. But do you hear those words? Are you listening to the Word? Do you believe what God is saying?

It can't be much plainer than this: If you belong to a church that believes the whole Bible, and you are sick but don't present yourself to the elders for healing, then you are in rebellion against the Word of God. The Bible has commanded you to call upon your elders, to receive their prayers and blessings, and to receive forgiveness for your sins. When you have done that, God bestows His power and authority for the healing of illness and disease.

Some believers are hurting, and some are in trouble or sick; yet, they never call the church. They're self-sufficient. They want to do it themselves, or they just want the doctors to take care of it. That's more common, more acceptable, less risky, even if it doesn't always work. But, brothers and sisters, you can't do this on your own. God has put elders in the church to minister to your needs, and He commands you to come to Him through them for your healing.

Anytime pride causes you to ignore the Word of God, you're not living by kingdom principles but by a mind-set of pride and doubt from the very gates of hell. And that kind of life simply cannot coexist with the life of the kingdom. We're not to be *independent*. We are to be *dependent* upon the Lord and fully united with Him through Christ our Lord.

I cannot help but think of the revelation that was given to the church when Peter saw Jesus Christ as the true Messiah and the Son of the living God. Christ asked him, "Who do men say that I, the Son of Man, am?" After Peter related what others had said about Him, he finally confessed the Lord's true identity, saying, "You are the Christ, the Son of the living God." No sooner had the words left his mouth than Jesus answered, "Blessed are you, Simon Bar-Jonah, for flesh and blood has not revealed this to you, but My Father who is in heaven. And I also say to you that you are Peter [the Greek word here is *petros,* meaning "a piece of rock"], and on this rock [in this case the Greek word is *petra,* or "a mass of rock"] I will build My church, and the gates of Hades shall not prevail against it" (Matt. 16:13–18).

Here is evidence that God has given us a piece of the kingdom. The disciple whose name had been *Simon Bar-Jonah* was renamed by Jesus as *Peter,* a stone or pebble. This verse makes it clear that Peter is to be a piece of the greater mass of stone that is the kingdom of God—the *petra.* And Jesus says that it is upon that truth that He will build His kingdom.

But He doesn't stop there. To make sure we know the context of what He is saying, Jesus says, "And I will give you the keys of the kingdom of heaven, and whatever you bind on earth will be bound in heaven, and whatever you loose on earth will be loosed in heaven" (v. 19). Jesus seems to be telling us that we are not the door of the kingdom—we merely hold the keys to the door. Jesus Christ is the door of the kingdom. If you are a citizen of the kingdom, you have the key to open the door so others may enter in to know their Savior and King.

You and I are not the door, we are not even the key, but we hold the keys to the kingdom. That is the kingdom life. Jesus says, "I will give you the keys of the kingdom." And you have Christ's authority, so that the things you bind on this earth will be bound in the eternal kingdom as well.

There is a revelation in verse 20. It says, "Then He commanded His disciples that they should tell no one that He was Jesus the Christ." How can that be? First Christ gives us authority to bind even the unseen forces of heaven, but He then forbids us from speaking of it openly? What was He trying to do? We have been given the key, but we cannot give that key to an unbeliever. He says tell no one!

Unless you are drawn by the Spirit of God, you cannot possess the keys of the kingdom. Christ has drawn only those to Himself whom He can entrust with the keys of the kingdom. When He says, "Tell no one," He means, "Don't tell those who are not walking in My kingdom how to use the keys."

Do we ever do that? Yes, we do. We bring people into the church who have never been saved or truly redeemed, and we teach them how to pray and how to preach. They take on the mannerisms of believers. Though they are not saved, they know how to pray. They even know how to praise the Lord. They know how to use all the biblical jargon. Christ warns that we are not to give the keys to the kingdom to such people until they are truly saved.

Kingdom Operations

Christ could have gone about telling people all the details of life in the kingdom, but instead He called a few disciples who had been with Him, who had known Him, and who recognized Him as the Son of the living God. He said, "Look, folks, upon this truth I am going to build My church, and I'm giving the keys to you. Got it?" What key was Jesus using? It was not a physical key but a revelation of the truth of the heavenly kingdom.

If you have this truth, you can open the doors of eternity, operate in the kingdom, speak the kingdom language, teach the kingdom life, and live to the fullest in the kingdom. But if someone tells you he loves God, but he doesn't even love his brother, then the Bible says that he is a liar. Anyone who does not love others is not truly a citizen of the kingdom, because God is love. If someone says he has kingdom power, but you don't see the power exhibited through the anointing of the Holy Spirit with the gift of tongues, the power to cast out demons, and the power to heal all manner of sickness, then either he is a liar or he is not using the kingdom power that God has entrusted to him. Because in the kingdom of God, you are to bear kingdom fruits.

When we operate in the kingdom, Satan doesn't know if it is us or Jesus speaking, because kingdom authority means he doesn't hear our voice but the voice of Jesus through us. We must be living, talking, and operating in the kingdom, and putting away everything that is of the world. We must put them out of our thoughts, out of the imagination. Put them away. For in the kingdom, God is sovereign. He is supreme. And if we are born again, renewed by the Spirit of God, then the authority we represent is also the highest.

As born-again believers who are walking in the Word of God, we are affiliated with God's supreme power and walking in such a way that no demon can stand before us! They are inferior to us because our lives are hidden in the kingdom of God. That is kingdom life. When we begin to walk in the kingdom of God or in the truth of God's Word, then we begin to walk with the One who is full of power, whose authority and ability can never be surpassed.

That is when we begin to see results to our prayers. When Peter, Paul, the apostles, and the disciples finally understood that Jesus Christ was the visible expression of the kingdom of God and that He was fitting them out with His own Spirit, they began to preach, heal, and baptize people into the faith with a power that was unprecedented in all of history. Even the power of Rome could not stand in their way.

They healed the sick and cast out demons. They built churches and preached the Word. They trained missionaries, and the gospel of Jesus Christ captured the entire world. Jesus said, "You shall receive power when the Holy Spirit has come upon you; and you shall be witnesses to Me in Jerusalem, and in all Judea and Samaria, and to the end of the earth" (Acts 1:8).

Was that really possible? Could it happen? History tells us that on September 18, in A.D. 384, the Christian faith did, in fact, become the official religion of the Roman Empire and eventually of the known world of that day. The eternal kingdom of God was spread and disseminated, at least for a space of time, through the rulers of this temporal world. The two kingdoms are not the same, of course, and should never be confused; but God was able at that time to use the power of this world to accomplish His divine purposes for spreading the gospel to the ends of the earth, just as Jesus had declared.

I Have Seen the Kingdom

Now, I want to ask you a question. Do you practice God's presence in your own life? Do you read His Word faithfully? Do you engage Him in conversations about critical issues that matter to you? Do you speak to Him in tongues? Do you repeat His Word to yourself and to those around you? I believe we should strive to possess those aspects of the kingdom if we are truly citizens of this kingdom.

If you constantly practice the presence of God by reading His Word faithfully and engaging Him in conversation, then you are feasting on the kingdom. For His Word is our bread, and communion with Him through prayer is the very water of the kingdom. If you practice these disciplines constantly, praying in the Spirit, then you will be operating in the kingdom. You will be fulfilling the covenant that God ordained when He said that we should write His law in our hearts and minds.

That covenant was a part of the work that Christ accomplished for us on the cross. He brought with Him a New Covenant that was superior to the Old Covenant that God had made with Moses. Christ Himself became the perfect sacrifice for our sins, and from that time and forever, no other deed, no other act, no other sacrifice could come close to what our Lord accomplished at Calvary. When Jesus rose from the dead on the third day, He gave us the living proof of kingdom life, setting the standard by which we are to live until He comes again.

Did that come as a surprise to the people of that day? Yes, it did. Were the people ready for what Jesus accomplished? No, they weren't. But they should have been. Some six hundred years before Christ, God spoke through the prophet, Jeremiah, saying:

> Behold, the days are coming, says the LORD, when I will make
> a new covenant with the house of Israel and with the house of
> Judah—not according to the covenant that I made with their
> fathers in the day that I took them by the hand to lead them
> out of the land of Egypt, My covenant which they broke,
> though I was a husband to them, says the LORD. But this is
> the covenant that I will make with the house of Israel after
> those days, says the LORD: I will put My law in their minds,

56

and write it on their hearts; and I will be their God, and they shall be My people.

—JEREMIAH 31:31–33

This is precisely what Paul is talking about when he writes that Jesus Christ obtained a more excellent ministry. The kingdom of God, revealed in our hearts and lives at the very hour of the Resurrection, is the ministry Christ came to accomplish on earth. Today the kingdom of God is still the ministry of Jesus Christ. If we are walking with Him, the kingdom is being revealed in hundreds of ways in our daily lives. We are supposed to continue in the ministry of God. If we continue in the ministry of God, we are continuing in the kingdom of God. The Bible says that Jesus became the mediator of a "better covenant." In other words, Christ came to preach the gospel of the kingdom, and He became the mediator of a better covenant, which was established on better promises.

Paul says, "But now He has obtained a more excellent ministry, inasmuch as He is also Mediator of a better covenant, which was established on better promises. For if that first covenant had been faultless, then no place would have been sought for a second" (Heb. 8:6–7). The old blood sacrifice was rendered obsolete by the Atonement of Jesus the Messiah. Paul goes on to say, "In that He says, 'A new covenant,' He has made the first [covenant] obsolete. Now what is becoming obsolete and growing old is ready to vanish away" (v. 13). Beloved, that has already happened. The Old Covenant is no more; the New Covenant is our daily reality.

If we really want to walk in things that are better, things that are more fulfilling than the Old Testament code, more than the dry and demanding context of the Mosaic law, then we must walk in Jesus Christ. The promises that He has given to us have already been established. They are beyond the covenant the Jews celebrate today.

The New Covenant is superior in every way because Jesus Christ established it on "better promises." If you have kingdom life within you, then you are standing on the promises that are better than any others. You can know for certain that the kingdom promises will never fail.

57

Part II:
Kingdoms in Conflict

4

The Kingdom Divided

JESUS WAS NOT shy about confronting those who didn't accept His witness. He didn't humor them with pleasantries and polite conversation; He spoke the truth, even when His words stung a little bit. On one occasion, when Jesus had healed a man who was blind and mute, a group of Pharisees approached and accused Him of breaking their law. He had driven an evil spirit out of the man, but the self-righteous leaders claimed that He was casting out devils by the spirit of Beelzebub, or Satan.

Jesus knew their thoughts, and He said, "Every kingdom divided against itself is brought to desolation, and every city or house divided against itself will not stand. If Satan casts out Satan, he is divided against himself. How then will his kingdom stand?" (Matt. 12:25). This may be a revelation for some people, but Jesus made it clear that Satan does have his own kingdom and is doing everything in his power to fortify it. His goal is to defeat the kingdom of Christ. It is true that every believer has authority over the forces of Satan, because Christ manifests His power in us. But Satan is working overtime to render us powerless, and he wouldn't divide his own forces for anything.

The same applies to the kingdom of God. God will not allow His kingdom to be divided. That's why the Bible says, "God is not the author of confusion" (1 Cor. 14:33). Once confusion exists in a kingdom, then the kingdom is headed for destruction. Once those who dwell in the kingdom argue, fight, and backbite against each other, once jealousy, anger, and envy break down the unity within the body, then the kingdom suddenly becomes a house divided. And a house divided cannot stand.

Jesus couldn't have said it any clearer. If Satan casts out Satan, then Satan's house cannot stand. By the same token, if those who have authority in the kingdom of God fight against each other, if those who are followers of Jesus Christ fight with their brothers and sisters in the faith, then we will become a disorganized and power-less force. That is precisely what happens when we allow physical, emotional, and theological differences to create factions within the church. We become a divided kingdom. Causing division is one of the most cunning tricks of the enemy, causing our forces to lose focus and effectiveness.

Jesus doesn't stop there. He goes on to say:

> And if I am empowered by the prince of demons, what about your own followers? They cast out demons, too, so they will judge you for what you have said. But if I am casting out demons by the Spirit of God, then the Kingdom of God has arrived among you. Let me illustrate this. You can't enter a strong man's house and rob him without first tying him up. Only then can his house be robbed! Anyone who isn't helping me opposes me, and anyone who isn't working with me is actually working against me.
>
> Every sin or blasphemy can be forgiven—except blasphemy against the Holy Spirit, which can never be forgiven. Anyone who blasphemes against me, the Son of Man, can be forgiven, but blasphemy against the Holy Spirit will never be forgiven, either in this world or in the world to come.
>
> —MATTHEW 12:27–32, NLT

This is such a rich passage, and there are several important things that we need to see in these words. First, we should notice that it is the Holy Spirit who empowers believers to do the work of the kingdom. Those who deny the power of God to perform the mirac-ulous are not just maligning those of us who believe in the power of miracles. They are also doubting the Holy Spirit and blaspheming against Him. Christ tells us such impiety can never be forgiven. He doesn't mince words. He says, "Anyone who isn't helping Me opposes Me, and anyone who isn't working with Me is actually working against Me." When we deny the power of the Holy Spirit in the kingdom, we are denying Christ.

Beyond these stern warnings, we need to see that there is always a kingdom to be obeyed in this world. We're all on one side or the other. If we choose to fulfill the law of the flesh and live in sin, denying the power of God, then we will be walking in the influence of the devil and living by the rules of his kingdom. If, on the other hand, we choose to live by the grace of God and the power of the Holy Spirit, then we will be walking in the kingdom of Jesus Christ and living under His authority.

God obviously wants you to come to His kingdom, but He doesn't want to have to drag you. He wants to touch you and to reach out to you in love. He has invited you into His kingdom by grace and by the testimony of the saints over many years. But Satan is not just inviting you, he's wooing you into his kingdom by promising you all the worldly pleasures your mind can imagine. He'll say anything, do anything, and promise you everything to appeal to you and sucker you into the kingdom of darkness.

THE KINGDOM OF MAN

UNFORTUNATELY, SATAN'S KINGDOM is not the only rival gang in town. There are some Christians around these days who have a kingdom of their own. At least they seem to think they do. Jesus tells the parable of the rich man, saying:

> The ground of a certain rich man yielded plentifully. And he thought within himself, saying, "What shall I do, since I have no room to store my crops?" So he said, "I will do this: I will pull down my barns and build greater, and there I will store all my crops and my goods. And I will say to my soul, 'Soul, you have many goods laid up for many years; take your ease; eat, drink, and be merry.'" But God said to him, "Fool! This night

your soul will be required of you; then whose will those things be which you have provided?"

So is he who lays up treasure for himself, and is not rich toward God.

—LUKE 12:16–21

There are many people in this country who are laying foundations in this way. They take personal credit for their successes and make plans for the future as if God were their silent partner. They believe it's God's job to make sure that everything comes up roses in their life. They seek fertile ground to bring forth a plentiful harvest and act as if it were God's job to make sure the barns are always full. They don't really want God's input, of course. They say, "I'll do it *myself*. I'll pull down my barns and build even greater ones." They have no idea what peril they're in because of their vanity and arrogance.

I've seen this in many of today's churches during the last several years. Based on a faulty understanding of Scripture, there are some who think they can exploit God's generosity for their own personal gain. In Luke 6:38 Jesus says, "Give, and it will be given to you: good measure, pressed down, shaken together, and running over will be put into your bosom. For with the same measure that you use, it will be measured back to you." In this important teaching from the Sermon on the Mount, the Lord tells us that we are not to hoard treasures on this earth but to give a tithe of whatever we have to the kingdom of God, so that those who serve in the household of God will not go hungry. But some Christians have decided that this passage, along with Malachi 3:10, gives them some kind of magic formula to use to exploit the rules of the kingdom for their personal gain.

They believe that the more they bless others, the more they will be blessed. So rather than using the blessings God has given them financially to build the kingdom, they exploit the kingdom of God by trying to use kingdom principles to advance their own material gain. Like the rich man, they daydream about their success, and say to themselves, "Soul, take your ease. Eat, drink, and be merry!"

Is this faith? Is this kingdom living? I say to you that it is nothing but lust and the love of money, which is the very root of evil. If you give a tithe to the church and to Christian ministries only so that you can gamble with God for a fat paycheck, then, my Christian friend, you need to reevaluate your motives while you still have time. You are trifling with very serious matters and tempting the judgment of God.

Those who are following this delusion use the Scriptures to tell people to get rich. But what are they really doing? They're building their own kingdoms, telling anyone who will listen how clever and smart they are to take advantage of this biblical principle. One man spoke to me a few years ago, telling me how he had built his business from scratch using this concept.

"When I started out," he boasted, "I was making twelve thousand dollars a year. But now I make over three hundred thousand dollars a year. I can go anywhere I want to go around the world. I have all the boats, planes, and automobiles I will ever need; I even have a great collection of classic cars." He was thrilled with himself. The whole time he was declaring these things to me, I could see that he was not really interested in the kingdom of God. He was too busy building his own kingdom.

When we spend that much effort building our own kingdoms, we lose sight of the kingdom of God, which is the only kingdom that matters. But, equally dangerous, when we lose sight of the kingdom of God, we become a prey of Satan, because he knows that one of the surest ways to win us over for his kingdom is by getting us to take our eyes off the kingdom of God.

Today there are people who are operating in their own kingdoms. Others have sold out—lock, stock, and barrel—to the kingdom of Satan. Some may even be Christians, moonlighting for Beelzebub or operating in their own little worlds.

It's very hard to shake such people loose from their delusions. They cry, "It's all mine! It's *my* kingdom, and this is what I have done, all on my own."

God's kingdom comes into our lives when we receive His Word. But Satan's kingdom doesn't come into our hearts—Satan's kingdom drives us to do things we never expected to do. He pushes us into places we never wanted to go.

I Have Seen the Kingdom

In Luke 12:22 we read, "And he said unto his disciples, Therefore I say unto you, Take no thought for your life" (KJV). Now, this doesn't mean we shouldn't plan for the necessities of life. But it does mean that we shouldn't be schemers. The world schemes, plans, and thinks so much these days, but believers don't have to do that. Whenever we start scheming and planning as if success were dependent upon our own logic, then we deny our dependence on the sovereignty of God. We start chewing our fingernails, worrying about this and that, and wondering how we're going to accomplish all our goals. God did not call us to plan and scheme for our own success. He called us to come to Him, to depend on His guidance, and to reason together with Him. If we really want to see things work out God's way, then we need to reason according to God's way, which is through His Word.

FIRST THINGS FIRST

HEAR THE WORDS of Jesus from a modern paraphrase:

> So my counsel is: Don't worry about things—food, drink, and clothes. For you already have life and a body—and they are far more important than what to eat and wear. Look at the birds! They don't worry about what to eat—they don't need to sow or reap or store up food—for your heavenly Father feeds them. And you are far more valuable to him than they are. Will all your worries add a single moment to your life?
>
> And why worry about your clothes? Look at the field lilies! They don't worry about theirs. Yet King Solomon in all his glory was not clothed as beautifully as they.
> —MATTHEW 6:25–29, TLB

In other words, which one of us can change our situation by doing things our own way and thinking our own thoughts? But isn't that how we try to do it most of the time? We think about it and worry continually, but Christ has already done the critical thinking for us. He calls us to follow Him and take no thought for tomorrow. It doesn't matter what I think. I am to let go of my goals

66

and ambitions and live by the Word of God.

That's hard for some people to accept. All their lives they've lived by their wits; that's the only way they know how to do things. Intelligent people always want to do their own thinking. That's why Jesus prayed, "I thank You, Father, Lord of heaven and earth, that You have hidden these things from the wise and prudent and have revealed them to babes" (Matt. 11:25). We are to think of God's Word and to live by His commands. We are not supposed to try to figure it out on our own. Doing it any way but God's way simply will not work.

Jesus says that you cannot add one inch to your height by thinking about it. If you are not able to do the most trivial things by yourself, then why are you trying to run the big things your way? Just stop for a minute and look at the flowers; look at the way they grow. They're beautiful and fragrant, but they don't work at it. They don't have to punch a time clock or put in overtime hours. And yet, Jesus says that even Solomon, the richest man in the world, never had it as good as those simple flowers of the field. Never!

According to the Word of God, King Solomon was the richest man who ever lived on the face of the earth. When the Queen of Sheba visited the courts of Israel, she said, "Everything I heard in my own country about your wisdom and about the wonderful things going on here is all true. I didn't believe it until I came, but now I have seen it for myself! And really! The half had not been told me! Your wisdom and prosperity are far greater than anything I've ever heard of!" (1 Kings 10:6–7, TLB).

Where did Solomon get his riches? From the same place as the wisdom for which he prayed—from God. The Bible says we should seek wisdom. But it also says that the fear of God is the beginning of wisdom. If you want to know God, or if you have the wisdom to seek Jesus Christ, you have something worth far more than gold or mere dollars. Solomon had material wealth. But he also had the wisdom of God.

Yet, in all of his glory, Solomon was no more blessed than the flowers of the field or the birds of the sky or anyone of us who knows and loves the Lord our God. When they wake up in the morning, the birds sing to the glory of God. The flowers burst forth in radiant bloom to the glory of God. "The earth is the Lord's and the fullness thereof" (Ps. 24:1, RSV). As these creations glorify their Maker, they are not in their own kingdoms, but they are in the kingdom of God. God cares for every one of them.

When we become citizens of the kingdom, we no longer need to bother ourselves with things that we're unable to handle. God will take care of it. When we sleep, we can sleep peacefully knowing that God will take care of us. When we work, we can work peacefully because God takes care of us. Of course, we must be responsible; we must do the things in our home and family and on the job that we're expected to do—and even to excel at it. Christ calls us to be honorable workmen, worthy of our hire, people of passion and drive—but we don't go around worrying about things that are better left in God's hands.

The Bible says that if we think we stand alone, we are going to fall. We can know that we stand if we're standing with God. And how do we know that? Because we reason with God and His Word; His Word tells us that if we receive Jesus Christ into our hearts by faith, we will be able to stand.

Ephesians 6:11 says, "Put on the whole armor of God, that you may be able to stand against the wiles of the devil." Galatians 5:1 says, "Stand fast therefore in the liberty by which Christ has made us free, and do not be entangled again with a yoke of bondage." If we receive Christ, we will have the strength to stand. But if we try to walk and work in our own kingdom, by our own rules, then we're bound to fail.

Jesus goes on to tell us, "If God so clothes the grass of the field, which today is, and tomorrow is thrown into the oven, will He not much more clothe you...? Therefore do not worry, saying, 'What shall we eat?' or 'What shall we drink?' or 'What shall we wear?' For after all these things the Gentiles seek. For your heavenly Father knows that you need all these things" (Matt. 6:30–32).

We are not citizens of the kingdom of this world, but we are citizens of His kingdom. We are His nation. We are His people. If that's the case, then we have all the privileges of His chosen ones. Satan, as we've seen, is the god of this world. He is the god of this world's system. If it seems like the world today is going to the devil, you shouldn't be surprised—it is his! The Bible says that the earth belongs to the Lord, and the fullness thereof, but the world system belongs to Satan, and he is trying to use that system to influence and overcome the kingdom of God.

We who are children of the kingdom of God must not fashion our minds after the things of this world. To do so makes us ungrateful citizens and unfit subjects of the eternal kingdom of God.

My Sheep Know My Voice

"Fear not, little flock," Jesus says, "for it is your Father's good pleasure to give you the kingdom" (Luke 12:32, KJV). When we talk about the kingdom, most Christians think we're talking about some faraway place. Even most preachers think we're talking about a kingdom in the sky, and we're just flying around in a holding pattern waiting to land in heaven. That's because they have failed to understand the kingdom.

The kingdom is a place of royalty. Yes, it is a glorious realm and a place of divine transcendence. But God intends to bring this kingdom into our lives at the precise moment that we say *yes* to His invitation. When we say the words, "Jesus, I receive You as my Lord and Savior," at that very moment, the reality of the kingdom comes to us. It is God's good pleasure to give us the kingdom.

In His kingdom, there is a life to be lived. In His kingdom, there is a language to be spoken. In His kingdom, there is a song to be sung. When Jesus was teaching the disciples how to pray, He said that when we pray, we are to tell the Father, "Thy will be done in earth." Not in this world, but, "Thy will be done in earth, as it is in heaven." In other words, bring to this earth the glory and power of the kingdom, because if God takes pleasure in me, then He will reveal to me those things out there that I need to know.

Jesus said to the disciples, "What is the kingdom of God like? And to what shall I compare it?" After a brief pause, I imagine, He went on to answer His own question: "It is like a mustard seed, which a man took and put in his garden; and it grew and became a large tree, and the birds of the air nested in its branches" (Luke 13:18–19).

I Have Seen the Kingdom

This was a graphic image that the people readily recognized. But He didn't stop with just one parable. He said again, "To what shall I liken the kingdom of God?" Surely by this time He had the crowd's attention, so He used another metaphor they could easily understand. He said, "It is like leaven, which a woman took and hid in three measures of meal till it was all leavened" (vv. 20–21). Here it is again: something that starts small but grows gradually and miraculously, multiplying itself over and over again. This image of leaven or yeast had been applied to them before in the Scriptures. So they understood Christ's words.

He gave them these two parables of the kingdom so they would know that, while they are the evidence of God's presence, the force that grows within them is divine and mysterious. It was as if He were saying, "I just want to show you the kingdom in terms that you will quickly understand."

"So," He continued, "the best way for me to explain the way of the kingdom is this. It is like someone taking a seed, going out to the field, planting the seed, watering it, and caring for it until the seed begins to grow and flourish. And when it is fully grown, he looks out and says, 'This harvest began as a mere seed, so small I could hardly see it in the palm of my hand. But now the seed has grown and multiplied; now its leaves fan out like a magnificent tree. It is so great that now the birds of the air take their rest in it.'"

This principle is illustrated by the leaven or fermented dough that a woman placed into three measures of meal; as yeast will always do when it is allowed to ferment, it leavened the whole loaf. In Matthew 16, Jesus had warned the disciples to beware of the leaven of the Pharisees and Sadducees. Later, in Galatians 5:9, Paul says that a little leaven leavens the whole lump. In these and many other places, believers are warned that the kingdom of Satan will grow and expand if we are seduced by it. We are to be on our guard against the wiles of the devil.

Jesus says the kingdom of God will flourish and grow wherever the Holy Spirit is allowed to work in our midst. If you mingle with the wrong crowd, you'll be destroyed. But if you mingle with the right crowd, with God's people, you'll be all right. The kingdom of God is powerful. The Greek word used here for 'leaven' is *zume*, which

70

means "to cause to ferment or boil up." That is, to cause to grow and expand from within.

The Bible says that Jesus went throughout all Galilee teaching in the synagogues and preaching the gospel of the kingdom. He healed them of all manner of illness and all kinds of disease. In other words, within the kingdom of God there is salvation. Within the kingdom of God there is healing. There is righteousness, peace, and life. The kingdom of God is not meat and drink, but righteousness and joy in the Holy Ghost.

RESIST AND CONQUER

IF YOU REFUSE to walk in the Word of God, you become a prey for the enemy. He will be able to come in anytime he wants and use you any way he pleases. But you do not have to succumb to the enemy or let him come in and dominate your life. When the multitudes came to hear Jesus teach, as we see in Matthew 13, He sat down with them and told them the story of the farmer who was sowing seeds to start a new crop.

Some seed fell by the wayside, and the birds came and ate them. Other seed fell on stony ground; when the sprouts started to grow, the roots were too shallow and had no solid attachment to the earth, so the sun scorched them and burned them up. Other seed fell among thorns, and before long the thorns choked them out. But some seed fell on the good earth and brought forth fruit. "Some a hundredfold and sixtyfold," Jesus says, "and some thirty." Then He says, "Whoever has ears to hear let him hear." (See Matthew 13:3–9.)

When Jesus finished the story, the disciples were too embarrassed to admit they didn't understand what He was talking about, so they said, "Lord, why do You always talk in parables?" They made it sound as if they were saying, "Jesus, those poor ignorant people can't follow You when You use parables!" But what they really meant was, "We don't get it either! So, what did the parable really mean?"

Imagine their reaction when Jesus said, "You have been permitted to understand the secrets of the kingdom of heaven, but others have not." Boy, that must have confused them! But Jesus continued, saying, "To those who are open to my teaching, more understanding will be given, and they will have an abundance of knowledge. But to those who are not listening, even what they have will be taken away from them. That is why I tell these stories, because people see what I do, but they don't really see. They hear what I say, but they don't really hear, and they don't understand" (Matt. 13:11–13, NLT).

Well, by this time Peter, James, and John must have been thoroughly embarrassed, because they weren't getting much of it either. Did that mean they weren't really kingdom citizens? No, but they needed a little help. Jesus then told them that one reason He taught in parables was because it was the fulfillment of Isaiah's prophecy, which says: "You will hear My words, but you will not understand; you will see what I do, but you will not perceive its meaning. For the hearts of these people are hardened, and their ears cannot hear, and they have closed their eyes—so their eyes cannot see, and their ears cannot hear, and their hearts cannot understand, and they cannot turn to Me and let Me heal them." (See Isaiah 6:9–10; 44:18.)

Even kingdom citizens need a little help now and then, and Jesus knew exactly what was going on in the minds of the disciples. He knew they were a little thick, but He gave them some reassurance and said, "Blessed are your eyes, because they see; and your ears, because they hear. I assure you, many prophets and godly people have longed to see and hear what you have seen and heard, but they could not" (Matt. 13:16–17, NLT).

Obviously, Jesus was talking about the kingdom of God. He was from the kingdom of God. He was operating by kingdom rules and speaking kingdom words. He was doing everything He had seen the Father do in the kingdom of heaven. We are supposed to do everything we see Jesus do. We're supposed to imitate Him. We become like Him. If we imitate Jesus Christ, we are empowered to do the things the Father requires us to do. As you begin to program your mind not to be in the kingdom of this world but in the kingdom of God, you will be operating and acting in the kingdom of God.

What was Jesus trying to teach with the parable of the sower? He says that someone went out to proclaim the Word of God. Some who heard the Word didn't receive it. Others received it, but when things started shaking, they got choked. There are many, many religious believers who are walking in their own kingdom and getting choked. When things go wrong in ministry, or when their ministry is not going the way they want, they back off. They get choked.

Some who hear the Word get all excited about the Good News and go into action, but as soon as the heat is on and the going gets rough, they say, "Man, I am not called for that! I'd better back off." You see how it works? This is why the disciples were concerned. Jesus said things they didn't understand. They didn't have the knowledge, spiritually speaking, to comprehend His message. But when they came to Him later and asked for an explanation, He made it all clear.

Do you know why it was given unto them to know the mysteries of the kingdom? Because they followed Jesus Christ. The word that drew them to follow Him was the word of the kingdom. But they did not understand. Isn't that true for us as well? There are many things we don't understand, but we are still walking in the kingdom.

When they confessed their ignorance, Jesus told them that it was given unto them to know the mysteries of the kingdom. Anytime we turn to God, we no longer have love for the kingdom of the world. We want to be with kingdom people and do kingdom things. We want to be in the kingdom of God. Suddenly we're not sold out to ourselves or to the world, but we're sold out to the kingdom of God. We begin to understand the things of God. We come to grips with the mysteries of the kingdom.

Those who have received the Word of God will have faith. The more we use our faith, the more faith we have. Our faith grows. Jesus said that to those who have, more shall be given. To those who do not have, what they do have already will be taken away from them. That is what is happening in the world today. Those who know the Lord are loving the Lord and growing in faith. They receive more of Him daily and are full of the Holy Ghost. For those who don't have the Lord, there is only misery. And what they have is being taken away from them.

Those who have spiritual gifts and begin to use them will see a multiplication of those gifts. To them more is given. But those who do not use the gifts they've been given will have their gifts removed, and their blessings will be diminished.

I Have Seen the Kingdom

As we begin to operate in the kingdom, we will see things the way Jesus saw them. The more we see things as God sees them, the more we will worship and praise His name the way He expects. Through worship and praise, He blesses us as He promised to do. Isn't that incredible? Isn't that a fantastic mystery? But now the secret has been revealed, and we should rejoice in what Christ has done, and is doing, in us, His chosen ones!

When Jesus told the disciples that the prophecy of Isaiah was fulfilled, He didn't say that everything in the prophecy would be revealed. He said that there are some who have eyes but can't see; some have ears but can't hear. Do you see it? Those who are hardened to the gospel will never see the glories of the kingdom. But those who have heard the gospel and believe will have even more. More sight will be given. Do you doubt that more was given to the apostles? Or to the disciples? No, because we have seen their works; we have read of them in the Scriptures. They were walking in the word of the kingdom, and they were filled with the power and the anointing of the Spirit of God.

Before the Ascension, at the end of His earthly ministry, Jesus told the disciples to go to Jerusalem and wait until they were given power from above (Acts 1:4–5). They didn't really understand what He meant, but they received His kingdom word. I am sad to say that most of the people I see in this country walk in their own kingdoms, and they want to operate in the kingdom of God. That is why we don't see miracles and wonders.

The kingdom comes into the heart, but if the heart is not receptive to it, our ears will not receive the kingdom. Some people's hearts are not prepared. But if we receive the word of faith and act upon it, we will be brought into the kingdom and into the mystery of God's eternal covenant. Faith comes by hearing and hearing comes by the Word of God. The only way a man can please God is by faith.

The writer of Hebrews says, "But without faith it is impossible to please Him" (Heb. 11:6). If you want to please God, then come to Him in submission, acknowledge Him as your Sovereign and Lord, and begin walking in His kingdom. When we receive the Word of God and begin to walk in faith, we turn away from every other kingdom in order to live forever in God's holy kingdom.

Just imagine how these words must have rung in the disciples ears: "Truly I say to you that many prophets and righteous men have desired to see the things you see and have not seen them. They longed to hear the things you hear but have not heard them. Hear, therefore, the parable of the sower." And He explained the parable once again in detail so they could understand and recognize that it was a word picture of the kingdom of heaven.

Just picture His disciples sitting with Jesus Christ and hearing Him say these things. They must have been nudging and elbowing one another, saying, "Did you hear what the Master just said?" I can see Peter scratching his head and leaning over to Thomas and saying, "Thomas, isn't that strange? I never realized what He was talking about *until now!*"

Jesus said that the prophets and the great men of faith desired to see these things, but they never got the chance. "That's us, Thomas!" Peter must have said. "And we're seeing it all! Hallelujah!" And they were actually hearing it from the lips of the One who would reign forever on the throne of David.

Those who were with Jesus Christ heard the Good News of the kingdom from His own mouth. They had the word from the King of kings. He was, and is, the One who sits on the throne. But we have heard it from the mouth of Jesus Christ as well. We who are alive and remain have heard the word of truth. We have heard Him when He said, "Come to Me, all you who labor and are heavy laden, and I will give you rest" (Matt. 11:28). He said, "Take My yoke upon you and learn from Me, for I am gentle and lowly in heart, and you will find rest for your souls. For My yoke is easy and My burden is light" (vv. 29–30).

If you will take that step today and come to Him, do you know what will happen? You will begin to operate in the kingdom, and all the goodness of the kingdom will flow through you. How do you do that? By seeking first the kingdom of God and His righteousness. By hearing the Word of God and responding to it, thus becoming a child of the King. Then our heavenly Father will see our needs, and He will meet them. That's His promise, isn't it?

The kingdom of God comes into our hearts. It exists in the heart of every Christian. But unless the Lord Jesus is reigning and ruling in our lives, we will be unable to claim the authority and the power that has been offered to us. Those who hear His voice but are preoccupied with the cares of this world or who are confused by envy and the deceitfulness of riches are like the seed that was choked out by thorns along the roadside.

It is not easy to walk in the kingdom. Greed, pride, and the scorn of the world work against us. Our envy and our mortal flesh work against us. The one who is controlling the kingdom of this world is the one who hates the kingdom of God—and that is none other than the devil himself.

Don't think you're fooling anybody by claiming to be independent. Sure, there are people who say, "Well, I don't want to waste time serving God right now, but I'm not going to serve Satan either. I just want to serve myself. I am a good person. I help other people when I can, I put a little money in The Salvation Army kettle, or I help the homeless in my town. I'm not a mean person. I never hurt anybody, and I'm nice to my family. I never kick the dog."

Those who are a little more pious may say, "I go to church every Easter, and I never curse." But Satan just smiles and says, "Yes, that's just what I'm looking for! Just keep building your own kingdom. I'll help you build it, just so long as you don't do anything to help build the kingdom of God." Satan will allow you to live for a time in the illusion that you can have your own kingdom. He will reward you and pat you on the back, giving you everything your senses desire, until it's too late to turn back to God. Then he'll slam the gate and lock it, and you will belong body and soul to him.

God says, "Come out from among them and be separate...Do not touch what is unclean, and I will receive you. I will be a Father to you, and you shall be My sons and daughters" (2 Cor. 6:17–18). Come out of Satan's clutches, come out of your lust and greed. Come out of your self-centered kingdom of the flesh into the kingdom of light! Let God add all those things that are missing in your life so that you can be blessed by your heavenly Father as a child of the kingdom.

Jesus says that the good seed are the children of the kingdom. But sown in among the children of God are children of the opposite kingdom. They are tares sown into the crop by the enemy. The enemy is the devil, and he sows these weeds in an effort to disrupt and destroy the harvest, which is the judgment that will come at the end of the world. At the time of the harvest, the good King will send His gatherers, the angels, to bring in the crop. Only then will God Himself separate the good wheat from the wicked and useless tares.

After the judgment is made by our Lord, the tares will be bound together and thrown into the fire; thus shall they ever be destroyed and flung out of the kingdom of God's holiness and goodness. The Book of Revelation tells us that the Son of Man, who is our King, Jesus Christ, shall send forth His angels. They shall call His kingdom out of the world, and He will judge the world, purge every evil thing, and purify the earth with fire.

Hear the words of Jesus when He says, "So it will be at the end of the age. The angels will come forth, separate the wicked from among the just, and cast them into the furnace of fire. There will be wailing and gnashing of teeth" (Matt. 13:49–50). Does that sound as horrible to you as it does to me? It should sound awful, because it is a true statement and a true warning from the very lips of our Savior who came, not to condemn the world, but that the world through Him might be saved (John 3:17).

When Christ has judged the wicked and cast them out of heaven, He says, "Then the righteous will shine forth as the sun in the kingdom of their Father. He who has ears to hear, let him hear!" (Matt. 13:43).

Is God unfair to condemn men and women to hell simply because they chose not to come into the kingdom? Absolutely not! He has been very fair. In fact, He has bent over backward to share the kingdom with all who will turn away from wickedness and come into the kingdom. The Bible says, "Let him that heareth say, Come. And let him that is athirst come. And whosoever will, let him take the water of life freely" (Rev. 22:17, KJV).

God has been more than fair with us by giving us the kingdom of His Son. The kingdom is like seed that is cast freely upon the earth. It is like dough that is mixed with common flour so that it might spread to all. The kingdom is the Word of God that comes to us, to draw us into the place where God wants us to be.

God intends for us to walk and talk like citizens of the kingdom.

I Have Seen the Kingdom

He wants us to act like citizens of the kingdom. If you set yourself up as a kingdom of one, then you are in open defiance of God's offer. He is not responsible for the choice you have made. He asks you to come in; He pleads with you cordially; He sent His Son to die for your sins so that you might be made free of the debt you have accumulated throughout your life. But if you refuse His offer, you have only yourself to blame if you spend eternity in the lake of fire.

God will never force you into His kingdom. But neither will He allow His kingdom to be divided. You cannot serve both God and mammon. If you refuse Christ's gift of life, then one day He will have to force you out, and that will be the worst and the longest day of your life—it will last for an agonizing eternity. So let those who have ears hear what the Lord is saying. Choose this day whom you will serve, whether you will serve the gods of this world or the One true God who has come that you might have life and have it more abundantly.

Start today, will you? Walk in the kingdom of God. Bow before Jesus Christ, right now, and inherit His free gift of eternal life!

5

The Kingdom United

SATAN HAS BEEN trying to establish his kingdom ever since he was thrown out of paradise in ages past. And he's still at it.

In the end, Satan's kingdom is no rival for the kingdom of God. It will not prevail. But over the centuries, this fearsome enemy of God and man, abetted by legions of willing co-conspirators and human allies, has built a vast empire in this world. Through vanity, arrogance, and sin, his empire has become one of the most powerful and compelling forces in the world today. Satan's kingdom wages war against the people of God. Allied with the powers of darkness is the kingdom of man, which is a kingdom of pride, selfishness, and personal ambition that stands in defiance of the kingdom of God.

Each of these kings is very real and very active in today's world—especially now as we are coming nearer to the End Times. The forces of God are working day and night to save those who will heed His voice and come to the cross of Christ. The forces of darkness are also working, sneering at the cross, scorning the work of the church, stealing souls daily from the kingdom of heaven.

The forces of man are working too, selling the lie that "you have to be true to yourself." You've heard all the litanies on the radio and television: "Be all that you can be!" "You deserve the best!" "You only go around once, so grab all the gusto you can get!" The humanist dream says that you are the captain of your fate and the master of your soul. Satan exploits these fanciful delusions to turn

79

men and women away from God.

Anyone who bites on these lies of the enemy shouldn't be surprised when he or she has to stand before God one day and hear Him speak those most horrible words: "I never knew you; depart from Me, you who practice lawlessness!" (Matt. 7:23). When that sentence has been pronounced by God, the person receiving that judgment will be cast into the lake of fire for all eternity, with no prospect of parole and no hope of mercy. It will be too late to repent.

God will not countenance competitors to His kingdom. Those who pay allegiance to any kingdom but His are only fooling themselves. They cannot serve themselves. If they think they're being objective and nonjudgmental by avoiding the kingdom of Christ, they are falling for a cruel and fatal trick. For in the end, God wins. Those are not my words. It's in the Bible. Just take a look at Revelation, chapters 19 and 20.

The power of God Almighty is the greatest force the world has ever known. It is greater than any earthquake, tidal wave, hurricane, volcanic eruption, or asteroid hurtling to earth from outer space. It's greater than any nuclear blast and greater than any creative or destructive force the mind of man can conceive. Greater, in fact, than all of them combined.

That's why the Bible says, "He who is in you is greater than he who is in the world" (1 John 4:4). When you give your life to Jesus Christ, you have that force abiding in you, and it is the very force of good. But when you make God your enemy, or when you allow Satan to benefit from your attitude of casual neglect, then the power of God moves against you. Surely no one in his right mind would ever want to be in that position.

TROUBLING TRUTHS

JESUS SAID SOMETHING very startling about this. He said, "Not everyone who says to Me, 'Lord, Lord,' shall enter the kingdom of heaven, but he who does the will of My Father in heaven" (Matt. 7:21). For all those who are of the opinion that the kingdom of God is some far-off pie in the sky, some figment of the imagination, or some never-never land for good little boys and girls, this is going to come as a shock to them: Jesus Christ came to establish the kingdom of God in our lives. And that's no fairy tale. You can get in or you can get out, but you can't ride the fence.

When we depart from this world at the end of our lives, we all inherit the kingdom we served in this life. Those who served the kingdom of God will inherit the kingdom of heaven, but those who served some other kingdom, regardless what they may have called it or how they may have thought of it, will inherit eternal separation from God. That is the inevitable result of serving any other kingdom.

If we want to do the will of the Father, then we have to begin by doing what Jesus asked us to do. If we do that, we will find that the kingdom of God is already in our midst. That's the promise of Scripture. When we obey Christ, we abide in the Father's kingdom. If we *seek first the kingdom* of God and His righteousness, then all the things we need to live victoriously in this life *shall be added* unto us. How much simpler can it be?

When we read the words, "Not everyone who says to Me, 'Lord, Lord,' shall enter the kingdom of heaven," we may think of the last days. We may say, "Sure, that's what it means. In the last days, at the Great White Throne Judgment, God is going to say that not everyone will be allowed to enter into the kingdom." Actually, Jesus means more than that. He is saying that the kingdom belongs to those who are doing the will of the Father right now, today, at this very moment. We are to apply this word to our lives today. If we are unable to take care of today, how can we take care of tomorrow?

Doesn't the Bible say that we are to take no thought for tomorrow? "Let God handle tomorrow," it says. That's His job. You don't have to wrack your brain to find out what's ahead of you. Unless God gives a specific word of knowledge or a word of wisdom, saying exactly what will happen tomorrow, then we are commanded to concentrate on what He has given us to do each day. Leave tomorrow for the prophets. As we have already seen, the Lord's prayer bears this out. Pray each day that God will "deliver us from evil."

If I seek after things that please God, I naturally begin to seek His righteousness. When I take care to live by God's Word, He will take care of my needs. Everything that I need as a human being will be added unto me. I have God's Word on that. I don't have to struggle and wonder how I'm going to make ends meet. My first concerns should be the building of God's kingdom, seeing God's people established and built up in the faith, and seeing lives won for Christ. These are God's priorities, and they should be our priorities as well.

Now I am seeking the things of God. Constantly, each day, my fondest hope is to do God's will. When I make up my mind to let God take charge of the big things, He lets me take charge of things within my own frame of reference. I remember one time when this idea came to me forcefully, in a way that really affected my thinking. Several years ago, while living in England, I was concerned about how I was going to make ends meet financially, and God showed me something I'll never forget.

He asked me, "Kingsley, how big is your pocket?"

I hesitated a moment to be sure I'd heard Him correctly. Then after a second I said, "Well, Lord, my pocket is not too big—only as big as the tailor makes it."

So then He said, "Well, Kingsley, how big is My pocket?"

"Oh, Lord," I said. "I don't know that! But Your pocket must be very large."

He said, "Put your hand into My pocket, Kingsley, and let Me put My hand in your pocket, and let's draw out whatever we find there." What an awesome thought, to put my hand in God's pocket and take out anything I wanted. But He also said, "Then I'll put My hand in your pocket, and I'll take anything I want."

Well, I have very small pockets. If God were to go into my bank account, He could only draw a little bit out of it. If He took everything I owned, it wouldn't amount to much. But I realized that God has a tremendous bank account. It's enormous! It's bigger than anything I could ever imagine.

As I thought about reaching into God's pocket, I suddenly realized that there were many things in His pocket that already had my name on them. Of course, I knew that He owns everything there is, but suddenly I saw that He has set aside many things for my good. In fact, He put them there just for me, to bless me, because I am His child.

What a stunning revelation! God had already earmarked some of the treasure in His pockets for my blessing. But why should that surprise me? What have I been saying all along? If I seek first the kingdom of God and make His kingdom my first priority in life, then everything that Kingsley Fletcher and his family will ever need will be provided. As the ministry and my work at Life Community Church in North Carolina continue to put God's kingdom first, putting all other claims and interests aside, then all our needs will be met. That's God's promise. This is the will of God in Christ Jesus concerning us. It is His plan.

You may be surprised to know that the word *faith* appears only twice in the entire Old Testament. But in the New Testament, it appears two hundred forty-five times, in two hundred twenty-nine separate verses. Does that surprise you? It surprised me when I first discovered it. But as I began to think about it, I realized that under the Old Covenant God didn't demand as much faith as He does now under the New Covenant.

God's revelation of Himself was very different under the Law, so His demands were different as well. Through the prophet Jeremiah God said, "I will put My law in their minds, and write it on their hearts" (Jer. 31:33). It was only then, with the revelation of the New Covenant in Jesus Christ, that *faith* would become a daily reality to believers.

But what about the other concept we find in the Bible, the word *believe? Believe* appears in the Old Testament just forty-five times, but in the New Testament it appears two hundred sixty-eight times. Another important word is *trust.* When the word *trust* is used in the Old Testament, it refers to belief and faith—they're inter-related. But the word *trust* is found one hundred fifty-four times in the Old Testament, while it appears only thirty-five times in the New Testament. Isn't that interesting? Why is there such an imbalance in these terms? I would suggest that it's a direct reflection of the types of worship that God demanded from His people at different times, based on His self-revelation under the Old and New Covenants.

Think about it. It is relatively easy to trust someone you can see with your eyes or with whom you have direct and immediate contact. It is relatively easy to believe in someone who is standing beside you. But it is another thing altogether to have faith in one whom you have not seen or experienced firsthand. If you have a father, it is easy for you to believe that he is your father. But it is another thing to have faith in him as a father.

You believe in someone because of what you see. The patriarchs and priests of the Old Testament prepared ritual sacrifices and approached God essentially face to face in the holy of holies within the tabernacle. The priests performed the sacrifice of humiliation and received forgiveness vicariously for the Jews. But Christ, who became our sacrifice, paid our debt of sin once and for all, and today we experience forgiveness through faith in Him.

Faith is not something we can see with our eyes. It is something we claim by a conscious mental act. It is the force of our sincere conviction that Jesus Christ is truly our Savior and Redeemer and that He made atonement for our sin on the cross of Calvary. Does that mean it is an emotional response? No question. Yet, Paul says, "Faith is the substance of things hoped for, the evidence of things not seen" (Heb. 11:1, KJV). Once we possess true faith, it is solid as a rock, and nothing can shake our belief. That's why these are such vital concepts for the Christian.

FAITH AT WORK

WHEN THE BIBLE talks about trust in the Old Testament, it is also talking about faith and belief. Many people in our world believe that God exists. Gallup polls over the last twenty years have shown that more than 90 percent of Americans believe that there is a God. If that's so, then why is our society in such crisis? Why is this country falling apart, being ripped apart by crime, violence, and sexual promiscuity? Is it because people don't believe that Jesus Christ is the Son of God? No, that's not it. Polls by the Barna Group and others show that a majority of Americans do believe that Jesus is God's Son.

They don't have any problem believing that. But they do have a problem placing their faith in Jesus as the Son of God and the Savior of mankind. They cannot do what the New Testament demands that all Christians must do: "Have faith in God" (Mark 11:22). They can't see Him as their personal Savior. Jesus assured Peter and the disciples that faith can move mountains; but if we turn our eyes away from the kingdom and seek after other treasures, then we are powerless, both in this world and the next.

The very moment we receive Jesus Christ as Savior and Lord, our old nature is taken away. We are converted. We put away unrighteousness, and the righteousness of God begins to operate in our lives. That's why Christians can say with confidence, "I can do all things through Christ who strengthens me" (Phil. 4:13). When we seek God's kingdom and His righteousness, we receive power from on high that enables us to do the work He is calling us to do at this moment.

We begin doing all the things that God allows us to do, and we leave the rest in God's hands. We do the things we can do, knowing that He will do the rest. But that is only true when we are willing to walk by faith—to walk in the light even as He is in the light. This is the power that Jesus Christ gives us through faith.

From time to time people who have seen or heard about the miracles God has performed in my life will come and ask me how it happens. A minister came to my home not long ago and asked me this question. He said, "I want to be frank with you, Dr. Fletcher, so I have to ask you a question. Please tell me how it is that God does all these wonders in your life. I have been to your church many times," he said, "and I have seen lives changed, families restored, and condemned cases repaired by God's love. How can this be? I want to know your secret!"

I knew what he was asking, but sometimes I don't want to tell people my secret. First, the power of the supernatural is not a secret to those who truly walk with God. It is not a secret to those who are living the kingdom life. But some people just want to get something for themselves from the Christian life so that they can gain the treasures of the kingdom without giving God what He really wants, which is their lives, love, and labor. Miracles, although a blessing, can sidetrack weak and vulnerable believers by placing their focus on people and their giftings rather than upon God.

They expect to learn—in one day, and with little or no personal sacrifice—what I've learned during more than fifteen years in ministry and a lifetime of Christian service. Are such people able to handle the mysteries of the faith? Can they be trusted with the secrets of the kingdom? Can they even understand it? I think it would be much better for them to follow Christ and seek these principles for themselves in the Word of God. If they are seeking God's *hand,* they must rather seek His *face.*

If God gave us access to the mysteries of the kingdom in one day, there would be no need to follow Him all the days of our lives. Some would say, "Now I have the treasure, so I'll go and do my own thing!" But God wants us to seek Him continually. We are to come after Him, take up our cross daily, and follow Him.

If you give a child a vast sum of money, she will not know how to handle it. Because she is immature and lacks experience, she will spend it on any whim that comes to mind, and the treasure will soon be wasted. But if you give her first a quarter, then a half dollar, then a dollar, gradually increasing the gift as she gains maturity, in time she will learn the value of a dollar and, hopefully, will learn how to be responsible with even much larger gifts.

A lot of Christians today expect God to give them everything they need all at once. They read the parts of the Bible that talk about God's good gifts and the powerful resources that God makes available to His saints, but they don't want to take the baby steps needed to build their strength and maturity. They fail to *seek first His kingdom and His righteousness.* But it doesn't work that way.

I explained this to my visitor, then I told him something else that he wasn't expecting to hear. I said, "To tell you the truth, my friend, I don't know how to operate the buttons of the kingdom. You see, I'm not the one who makes things happen. I don't do miracles."

I explained that miracles happen because I am seeking God's kingdom and His righteousness, and it is His plan to make available to me everything that I need for this life. The Bible says, "Surely goodness and mercy shall follow me all the days of my life." That is what God is doing. Glory to God! "And I will dwell in the house of the Lord forever" (Ps. 23:6, KJV).

Then I said, "Are you prepared to dwell in God's house forever? Then you must seek first His kingdom and His righteousness. Those who receive the gifts of power will see their works confirmed by God through signs and wonders. That is the Word of God. In Hebrews we see that those who followed the Savior received a holy anointing: 'God also bearing witness both with signs and wonders, with various miracles, and gifts of the Holy Spirit, according to His own will' (Heb. 2:4)."

Signs and wonders follow those who believe on His name. They are entrusted with power from on high. Hebrews 11:1 says that faith is the substance of things hoped for and the evidence of things not seen. By faith the elders obtained a good report. By faith the worlds were framed out of nothing, by the word of God alone. In other words, God spoke the universe into existence by His word. Now this is something that the natural mind cannot comprehend.

But the most important concept can be seen in Hebrews 11:6, which says, "Without faith it is impossible to please Him, for he who comes to God must believe that He is, and that He is a rewarder of those who diligently seek Him."

Do you hear that? We will not be able to please God until we have faith. How do we get that kind of faith? Romans 10:17 says, "Faith comes by hearing, and hearing by the word of God." If you don't hear the Word of God, then guess what? You won't have anything with which to please God. Without faith it is impossible to please Him. The faith that comes into our lives is something from "out of nowhere." It means claiming and taking hold of things that you believe to be true even though the physical evidence may say that they don't exist. Your senses may tell you it's impossible, but with God, all things are possible.

Most people living in our world today do not understand faith. They live by *hope.* They hope things will turn out all right—and that's not faith. They can't really understand faith because faith comes *by hearing the Word of God* and by knowing that God is working everything out for the good of those who love Him and are called according to His purpose (Rom. 8:28).

Faith, Not Feelings

EVEN THOUGH WE have a living hope, a believer doesn't live by hope. Our hope is the imminent return of our Lord and Savior,

Jesus Christ. But as long as we live on this earth, our walk with Him is done by faith. We know that without faith it is impossible to please God. The New American Standard Bible says, "Now faith is the assurance of things hoped for, the conviction of things not seen." The Living Bible says, "What is faith? It is the confident assurance that something we want is going to happen. It is the certainty that what we hope for is waiting for us, even though we cannot see it up ahead."

No matter how you translate it, you cannot escape the essential message: Faith is the realization in real time of the things that we hope for through prayer and supplication. Faith gives us title deed to things we anticipate expectantly by trusting in Jesus Christ. Many of us find it so hard to have faith in the Word of God, even though faith started working in our life the very moment we said, "Lord, I am willing to let You be the boss of my life."

In Hebrews 11:3 we read, "By faith we understand that the worlds were framed by the word of God, so that the things which are seen were not made of things which are visible." Here and in many other places we see that God has tremendous power, and He has spoken worlds into existence. Yet we find it hard to see Him move and work in our lives because too often we hold back our faith and belief. We resist. We don't trust Him, and we fail to release our hearts to Him through faith.

Do you understand what these biblical writers are saying? The worlds were framed by the word of God so that the things we see with our eyes were not made from substances we can see with our eyes; they were formed by the spoken word of God. Now, tables and chairs were made by things that do appear. In fact, the pages of my Bible were made of things that do appear—they're made of paper. But God made the universe from nothing. He spoke, and it suddenly came into being. If a person says, "I believe in God," what that person is saying is this: "I am taking hold of this divine truth even though my eyes cannot convince me of it."

If you are saved today, it is because the Word of God was preached to you, and you believed on the name of Jesus Christ through faith. But if there were no Bible, the Word of God could not be preached. The Bible is the tangible revelation of God's Word in written form. It is His gift to us, for our good. Faith goes beyond just what we can hold in our hands. It is the essence of reality, but it is unseen.

If we have such confidence in God that we can trust Him implicitly and entirely, then we can attain to all the needs of this life. If we totally depend on almighty God and look to Him for our well-being, then we will not lack any good thing. The enemy will try to divert our attention. He always tries to take our eyes off the Father and make us believe that God's Word doesn't really work or that it doesn't apply to us. But remember, Satan is a liar and the father of lies.

How many people believe that God's Word is living and powerful and sharper than any two-edged sword? Everyone will say he believes it. We can go into any church and find that the people there go to church because they believe there is a God. They believe that Jesus Christ is the Son of God. But many of them do not really have faith in God. Remember what Jesus said in Mark 11:22? He said, "Have faith in God." But how can I have faith in God if I have not seen God?

People who teach evolution or any of the other humanistic beliefs that exalt mankind and deny the reality of God are trying to convince you that everything that exists came out of something that existed before. They can't accept the fact that God made the worlds out of nothing. Not just our world, but all the worlds in the universe. There are many worlds, and God made them all, billions of them, in galaxies scattered farther in space than the most powerful telescopes can reach. He made them all out of nothing!

For us to be able to attain to all our human needs, we have to go beyond just believing in platitudes. We can just say we trust in the cross of Calvary. There is faith unto salvation, and that is the essential first step. But those who seek first the kingdom of God and His righteousness have a type of belief that comprehends the might and majesty of God and the power by which He created the sun, the moon, and the stars.

Faith does not have to see before it believes. Faith laughs at impossibilities. It counts things which, through natural logic, cannot be done as done. When we pray, we come before God with confidence, but we leave the place with feelings of joy and fulfillment. People come before God with faith, but they leave God's presence secure in the knowledge that God has heard their prayer.

Most of us have problems with faith at some time or other, but we need to know that, although faith touches our feelings and emotions, it does not consist of feelings or emotions alone. If I pray for something, it doesn't matter how much I feel it. My emotions aren't going to bring the answer I desire. I have to know for a fact that I am trusting and depending on the Word of God, even when my eyes have not seen what I desire. My heart believes that it is going to come.

There are many Christians who are praying for their relatives and families to be saved. Others are praying for healing. They have prayed and prayed and prayed. But they leave their prayer closet with feelings. They say, "I feel it is going to be done." But when their feelings fail them, what happens? They walk away in disappointment. Some may say, "I trusted God. I put all my faith in Him, and He did not answer me."

The problem is not that God didn't answer but that they left their prayer room with feelings, not faith. If they continue in faith, God will honor His Word. You don't have to believe you're healed only because the pain is gone. You don't have to believe that you're saved only because you feel forgiven. You don't have to feel you have answers only because things are going smoothly. Instead, faith says, "I simply believe what God's Word says."

Just because the pain is gone doesn't necessarily mean that you're healed. You can feel forgiven without truly being saved. Things may start going smoothly for you, but that does not necessarily mean that God has given you the answers you want. Don't let feelings interfere with faith. You need to believe that anything you ask the Father in the name of Jesus will be done, not because you can feel it, but because He says it! And His Word is true.

Whenever attitudes are controlled by feelings, faith grows weak. Consider the case of a man I know who has prayed fervently for healing from a serious illness. After a time of intense and passionate prayer he felt he had a close encounter with God. He said, "I feel that everything is going to be all right!"

For the next several weeks he based his faith on his feelings. But then, six weeks later, his doctor told him the sickness was back. He worried, cried, and prayed harder than ever, but six weeks later he lost his faith in God and fell into sin. In just a few short months, this man, who felt he had a word from God, ended up worse than before.

I asked him, "Where is your faith?"

He said, "I don't know. Maybe God is using this to test me."

No, God wasn't using the illness to test him. The problem was that his faith was based on feelings. If you pray and believe that God's Word says it and that God is going to answer it, then don't jump in and try to help God out with your feelings. Just pack up your feelings, stand back, and watch what God can do! He wants you to depend totally on His Word. Believe that He has the power to do whatever He promised He would do.

BEARING WITH THE WEAK

GOD DOES NOT want you to be weak in faith; He wants you to be strong. He doesn't want you to be dead; He wants you to live. He doesn't want the devil to rule you; He wants you to reign with Him. Therefore, God is extending strength to you so that you may be strong instead of being weak in faith. But how are we to react to those who may be weak in faith? Are we to cast them out and reject them? Certainly not! We are to receive them.

Take a look at Romans 14, where Paul discusses the concept of Christian liberty.

> Accept Christians who are weak in faith, and don't argue with them about what they think is right or wrong. For instance, one person believes it is all right to eat anything. But another believer who has a sensitive conscience will eat only vegetables. Those who think it is all right to eat anything must not look down on those who won't. And those who won't eat certain foods must not condemn those who do, for God has accepted them. Who are you to condemn God's servants? They are responsible to the Lord, so let him tell them whether they are right or wrong. The Lord's power will help them do

as they should. In the same way, some think one day is more holy than another day, while others think every day is alike. Each person should have a personal conviction about this matter.

—ROMANS 14:1–5, NLT

Not everyone among us will be equally strong in faith. Obviously, in a growing church that will be the case. But we are not to separate out those who have less faith, and we are not to argue with them over their understanding of difficult spiritual issues. God understands that we may be weak in faith, and He makes allowances for our understanding based on the faith we have attained.

The passage goes on to say that there may be disagreements over what Christians are to eat or perhaps over which day of the week is the best day for worship. We may have strong opinions on these matters, and some will be better informed than others, but we should not allow these doctrinal issues to divide us from the essential importance of worshiping our Lord and Savior, Jesus Christ, and keeping His commandments.

If someone is weak in faith and is walking according to the things of his nature, I shouldn't despise that person. In fact, I have to receive that person and even honor him. Whether you eat or not, it doesn't make any difference. We know that. But if the person who has weak faith sees you doing something questionable, he may doubt and turn away from God because of your behavior. That's the real point. Paul says, "Preach the word! Be ready in season and out of season. Convince, rebuke, exhort, with all longsuffering and teaching" (2 Tim. 4:2). Reason with those whose faith is weak and bring them along, encouraging them in the faith so that they may grow stronger.

As Jesus gathered with His disciples for the Last Supper, He spoke with Peter, indicating that Peter's faith would be tested. Jesus said to him, "I have prayed for you, that your faith should not fail; and when you have returned to Me, strengthen your brethren" (Luke 22:32). Our Lord recognized that Peter would stumble, but He also knew that he would seek forgiveness and return to Him, growing stronger because of this testing. So He admonished Peter to use his experience to strengthen the others, so that they too might grow stronger in their faith.

We are told that the strong ought to bear the infirmities of the weak and not just to please themselves. "Let each of us please his neighbor for his good, leading to edification. For even Christ did not please Himself; but as it is written, 'The reproaches of those who reproached You fell on Me.' For whatever things were written before were written for our learning, that we through the patience and comfort of the Scriptures might have hope" (Rom. 15:2–4).

In the Word of God, you read about great heroes of the faith who failed and were restored and about those who perfected their faith through adversity and testing. All those things, Paul says, teach us patience, and they give us comfort and hope. It is not always a hope that things are going to be all right, but rather a hope that is based on the principles of God's Word. Not a hope that God is going to give you everything you want, but the hope that comes from knowing He will never leave you nor forsake you; He will always be as close to you as your own heartbeat. It is the hope of reassurance.

If someone is weak in faith and you are strong, then you are to receive that person. Can you think of practical applications for this teaching? Think for a moment of the disputes you've heard over the "order of service" in today's churches.

How are we to worship God? Are suits and fancy dresses the only attire we can wear to the house of God? Is it all right to have organ music? What about an orchestra or a band? Do they speak in tongues in your church? Are the sick healed? Do they dance in the aisles under the anointing of the Spirit of God? How is the sacrament of communion observed? How are members admitted? What is the correct manner of baptism? Can a man drink wine or smoke cigarettes and still be a Christian? Now, obviously, you see that all of these are hotly debated topics in our churches today. So what does the Bible say?

We must always remember that if we are strong, we have to let go and help the one that is weak. We are not to please ourselves, but we should please our brother or our sister. Now that is how faith is. Faith is not pleasing ourselves. If we are pleasing ourselves, we are going by our feelings. We need to please God. And we do please God by taking hold of His Word, trusting Him for what He said He would do, and doing what His Word says to do. Without faith it is impossible to please Him.

The Bible says that those of us who are strong are to receive those who are weak. This means a number of things.

First, it means that Christ desires for the church to be founded on love and understanding.

Second, it means that there are some who are weak in faith, and that in itself is no sin.

Third, it means that there are some who are strong in faith, but they are not to use their strength to judge and belittle those who are not as strong.

In this context, I think especially of Paul's words to the church at Rome, where he says, "I long to see you, that I may impart to you some spiritual gift, so that you may be established—that is, that I may be encouraged together with you by the mutual faith both of you and me" (Rom. 1:11–12).

Do you appreciate the tone of those words? Paul is saying, "I know that many of you are new Christians, weak in the faith, and without much experience in the ways of the church. Therefore, I long to see you soon so I can build you up in the faith and teach you what I have learned through my years of study and the ministry of the Word. I do not want us to have three or four different ideas about how to worship God; I want us to have a mutual or common faith between us, so that we may share in the spiritual gifts that God wishes to bestow upon His church." Do you see that?

Paul recognizes that there are some who have a weak faith. This is a kind of faith that constantly limits the personal benefits and privileges of the believer. It is a faith that denies the power of God and focuses on the "Thou Shalt Nots" instead of the "Thou Shalts." Basically, it is a faith that comes from wrong or inadequate teaching. It is not the kind of faith that can endure testing. It is not a strong faith.

Paul desires to share his spiritual gifts with them so that they might grow in the grace and knowledge of our Lord and Savior, Jesus Christ.

CHARACTERISTICS OF FAITH

STRONG FAITH REFUSES to be defeated. Strong faith endures hard circumstances. Strong faith always stands against outward appearances. It stands against what the human mind says or what the human eye sees. Strong faith stands against feeling and looks to the Word of God for strength. God expects every believer to have strong faith, but He gives us room to grow.

There are too many hot and cold Christians today. When some believers have problems their faith goes flat. As long as everything is going along smoothly, they say, "Boy, my faith is like a rock! I've really got it!" They act as if their faith were seven feet high! Why? Because everything is going smoothly. They have money in the bank, they have faithful friends, their children are doing all right in school, and everybody in Sunday school knows their name! But that's not the test of faith, is it?

A truly strong faith will stand up to adversity. It will not back off when everything falls apart and the tables are turned upside down. The devil always tries to counterfeit our faith. He brings doubt and unbelief. He tries to get us to depend on our feelings. Anytime he gets us into those areas, our prayer life is affected. If we fall for his trap, we can't pray effectively, and we no longer believe God for answers. That's when we have to say, "Satan, you listen to me, you old deceiver. Don't talk to me. God is on the throne of my life, and I'm not buying any of that stuff. So get behind me, devil. Be gone!"

We must tell him, "Satan, my faith is built on solid rock, and I trust the Word of God. I know that John 3:16 tells me I have been saved. Jesus lives in my heart, and you know it! So back off." If we let him get to us and start playing with our minds, Satan will confuse our feelings and emotions. He'll tell us that we've failed God and lost His blessing. Has he done that to you yet? He will. It's a common trap that Satan lays for believers.

When he tries that, just say, "Satan, my feelings don't tell me anything. My faith tells me all I need to know. I am a child of God, redeemed by Jesus Christ, my Savior, and filled right up to the top with the Holy Spirit! So scat, you weasel!"

Strong faith will not fall for the wiles of the deceiver. Also, it will never take *no* for an answer. The world comes so hard against us sometimes that we are tempted to say, "I can't take it anymore! I give up." But strong faith will never give up. It says, "I am determined to go with God. I am determined to serve the Lord. I will not give in to sin." That is strong faith. We may have no idea how we're going to do it, and our feelings may tell us to throw in the towel, but faith clings to the Word, to God's promises, and it perseveres through every adversity.

The Bible says, "Thou wilt keep him in perfect peace, whose mind is stayed on thee: because he trusteth in thee" (Isa. 46:3, KJV). Isn't that beautiful? I love the sound of those words, but even more I love what they say. God promises to keep all those who trust in Him in perfect peace because their hearts and thoughts are focused continually on Him! My friends, if you want a tip on how to have a strong and durable faith, I can't think of a better place to start. Focus continually on Him—seek *first* His kingdom—and you will be filled with the peace of God.

I have to believe what the Word of God tells me, and I must never take the word of the enemy. I will get rough with the enemy anytime he tries to interfere in my relationship with my God. I will be stubborn toward him. He will sneer, "Oh, you poor fellow, you just think God hears your prayers. How foolish you are!"

But I will say, "Okay, listen to me, devil. I don't *think* He hears my prayers. The Word of God says, 'I will look to the Lord; I will wait for the God of my salvation; my God will hear me' (Micah 7:7)." Jesus told us that "men always ought to pray and not lose heart" (Luke 18:1). That is strong faith. Strong faith is fully persuaded that God is able to keep His Word, and He will do it.

The Bible tells us that Abraham "did not waver at the promise of God through unbelief, but was strengthened in faith, giving glory to God, and being fully convinced that what He had promised He was also able to perform. And therefore 'it was accounted to him for righteousness'" (Rom. 4:20–22).

In another place, Paul says, "I know whom I have believed and am persuaded that He is able to keep what I have committed to Him until that Day." And then he adds this word of encouragement, saying, "Hold fast the pattern of sound words which you have heard from me, in faith and love which are in Christ Jesus" (2 Tim. 1:12–13).

To be fully persuaded, like Abraham, means to have a resolute and abiding faith. It means standing strong. Abraham was extremely convinced that God had said he would have a son, and that old man was going to take God at His word. He got confused when it didn't happen immediately, and he made mistakes. But he never doubted that God would keep His word. That's what we need, too. To walk in the kingdom of God and to attain all that God has ordained for us, we need a faith that is strengthened by feeding daily on God's Word.

When Jesus was in a storm on the Sea of Galilee, He spoke and the wind grew silent and the waves were immediately calmed. How did He do that? I will tell you. By faith. He was asleep in the bow of the boat, remember? Well, you might say His disciples were still in seminary at the time, still learning how to have strong faith—but, frankly, they were terrified. Some of these guys were lifelong fishermen, but that didn't matter. They were terrified. They thought they were going straight to the bottom of the sea!

They cried out to Jesus in alarm, and He said, "Why are you afraid, oh, you of little faith?" If we are believers and have been filled with the Holy Spirit, one of the only ways we can be a person "of little faith" is if we allow fear to control our emotions. The Bible says that if we entertain fear, our faith will be diminished. We believe the Word of God, but fear comes in and steals our joy. It's like having no faith at all. We fail to live by faith because we are controlled by an irrational fear.

We get another view of this situation in Matthew 14 when Jesus walked on water. Remember this tremendous miracle? If ever there was a demonstration of dynamic faith, this was it. The passage says:

> Now in the fourth watch of the night Jesus went to them, walking on the sea. And when the disciples saw Him walking on the sea, they were troubled, saying, "It is a ghost!" And they cried out for fear. But immediately Jesus spoke to them, saying, "Be of good cheer! It is I; do not be afraid." And Peter answered Him and said, "Lord, if it is You, command me to

come to You on the water." So He said, "Come." And when Peter had come down out of the boat, he walked on the water to go to Jesus. But when he saw that the wind was boisterous, he was afraid; and beginning to sink he cried out, saying, "Lord, save me!" And immediately Jesus stretched out His hand and caught him, and said to him, "O you of little faith, why did you doubt?" And when they got into the boat, the wind ceased. Then those who were in the boat came and worshiped Him, saying, "Truly You are the Son of God."

—MATTHEW 14:25–33

Peter saw Jesus walking on the sea, and he was stunned. The kids would say he was blown away. He couldn't believe it. No doubt he was afraid; after all, he thought it was a ghost at first. But you know Peter—he was a bull in a china shop. He yells out, "Is that You, Jesus? If that's You, let me come to meet You—on the water!"

So Jesus said, "What are you waiting for? Come on!" With a lump in his throat, Peter steps out of the boat, and you better believe that took some faith. He didn't look at the boisterous waves; he looked at Jesus. He just obeyed the command to come. And Peter walked on the water. But then he glanced down at his feet, and he thought, *Man, what am I doing out here! I must be crazy. This is water I'm walking on! You can't walk on water!* And suddenly, as the doubt set in, he started to sink. Finally Jesus pulled him out of the sea, put him back in the ship, and asked the question that Peter would think about the rest of his life: "Why did you doubt Me, Peter?"

UNITED IN FAITH

FOR ALL THE embarrassment Peter must have felt at the time, we can learn an important lesson from his experience. Faith that doubts is not faith at all, because it wavers and snaps under pressure. A wavering faith is of no value to the Christian. To have a vibrant and meaningful faith, we all need to lay hold of the words of Hebrews 10:23, which says, "Let us hold fast the confession of our hope without wavering, for He who promised is faithful." The King James Version expresses it best with the words: "Let us hold fast the profession of our faith without wavering; (for he is faithful that promised)."

If we truly believe that God is faithful and reliable, which He is, then we have no need to worry. Doubt can have no place in our thoughts when we trust Him completely. James says that a double-minded man is unstable in all his ways and can receive nothing from God (James 1:7–8). So let us hold fast the profession of our faith, without wavering.

Remember Christ's words? If we have faith and do not doubt, we can move mountains. We all need to move mountains from time to time, and God is always faithful. That's why He promised He would always be with us. He is the security service that stands behind the promises of the Word—and He is as good as His Word. In Hebrews we read: "For He Himself has said, 'I will never leave you nor forsake you.' So we may boldly say: 'The Lord is my helper; I will not fear. What can man do to me?'" (Heb. 13:5–6).

Whenever we reject the kingdom of this world, the kingdom of Satan, and the kingdom of man, we will be tested. But my challenge to every believer is that we should grow in the grace and knowledge of our Lord, feed daily on His Word, and stand firm in our hour of testing so that we may gain the kingdom of heaven. That is our blessed hope.

Be stubborn with the enemy when he comes knocking. Recite the Word of God to him, just as Christ did in the wilderness, and send him packing. He cannot stand that kind of rebuttal. Wherever God's Word prevails, Satan's kingdom fails. And when we build our foundations on the Word, we are building the kind of faith that pleases God.

Do you see the power that comes through confidence in the Word of God? This is how the kingdom grows strong. This is how the forces of darkness and division are subdued and defeated. When we all do these things, the kingdom of God is united and powerful. And the gates of hell shall not prevail against it!

6

Advancing in the Kingdom

WE HAVE SEEN how Satan has been trying to establish his own kingdom out of pride, and because he has allied himself so successfully with the vanity and arrogance of mankind, we have also seen that Satan's kingdom has become one of the most powerful forces in the world today. Pride fights against the kingdom of God. When men and women reject God's kingdom and give priority to erecting their own kingdoms, they unwittingly become a part of Satan's scheme, waging war against God.

The theory that best describes this apostasy of arrogance is what we know as the modern philosophy of humanism. It is a theory that exalts man and denies the power and authority of God Almighty. Humanism celebrates what I can do, what I can become, what I can build, and what I can create. It exalts all things human and removes God from the equation. Jesus, above all, is rejected, because faith in Christ means that we have to confess our frailty, sin, and failure before God. In its blind determination to exalt the merely human and mundane, humanism denies any allegiance to God.

The humanist believes in the essential goodness of man. He believes that if we could just perceive the natural goodness in the human heart, we would see that we are all gods—that the nobility, beauty, creativity, and inventiveness within us prove that we must be divine. Do you see what's happening here? The humanist accepts everything that exalts his own kind but denies the greater glory of his Creator. Do you ever wonder why some scientists, scholars, and intellectuals of our day seem so determined to resist the Christian faith? It's very simple. If God is real, and if He's really there, then the humanist's dream is a terrible lie.

Now I am one of the first to recognize and appreciate all the marvelous things that men and women have accomplished in the arts and sciences. There is no question that we humans are incredibly inventive and resourceful creatures. The advances in technology over the last hundred years are truly awesome—they are miracles of modern science. Our ability to penetrate the mysteries of the universe can be spellbinding. So please understand that I am not condemning all human endeavor. I applaud it. I have tremendous respect for what we call the "humanities." I am not condemning "humanitarianism," either, which means doing good for others through charity and benevolence. But I am very much opposed to the philosophy of "humanism," which, at its root, is a false theology.

ADVANCING IN FAITH

As WE SAW in an earlier chapter, Satan is only too happy for us to build our own kingdoms, because every kingdom that is not of God is an adversary kingdom and a hostile principality. He's all for that. But whether or not you believe what God says, and whether or not you accept what I'm going to say about these things, the kingdom of God is real. It is alive and working today. The kingdom of God is the most powerful force known to man. That's why the Bible says, "He who is in you is greater than he who is in the world" (1 John 4:4). But the force of Satan is working, too. And it's just as real.

Jesus Christ came to establish the kingdom of God in our lives. If you know anything at all about the Christian faith, then you know that when we depart from this world, Christians expect to go to a place of eternal peace and joy—a place we call heaven—where we will be citizens of God's eternal kingdom. Even pagans know that concept of faith. What they don't know, however, is that right now, today, the kingdom of God has been brought into the lives of all people who love God and are called according to His purpose (Rom. 8:28).

Advancing in the Kingdom

If we do what Jesus asks us to do, then we will be doing the will of the Father. And guess what happens then? We begin advancing in the Father's kingdom. That is, we *seek first the kingdom of God and His righteousness,* and then, as I have said over and over in these pages, all the things we need to live a prosperous and joyous life shall be added unto us. Isn't that simple?

Do we really want to advance in the kingdom of God? In our marriages, our jobs, and our faith, do we have the commitment to advance in whatever we do? I'm a hyperactive person. I hate to sit still. I hate being stopped in my tracks, not going anywhere. I'm the kind of person who would rather go somewhere and be lost than sit around waiting for something to happen. I think there's an important analogy here, because, as Christians, we're supposed to be advancing in the faith and not sitting around waiting for whatever comes along.

When we live in the Word of God, we are supposed to advance. Any person who cannot advance cannot be trusted. The person who is not advancing in the faith is full of excuses. One of the most diabolical conspiracies against advancement is the all-too-common excuse, "I'm waiting for the perfect time." Have you heard that one? Or how about: "I don't like the way that's being done. If I can't do it my way, then I'm not going to do anything at all." Sound familiar?

Jesus Christ was very much aware of people's attitudes and behaviors. He observed the way they gave their tithes and offerings in the temple. He took His disciples to the church, watched what was going on, and said, "Do you see the ones who are giving more than anybody else?" He pointed to a group of rich Pharisees and noted that they were giving out of their abundance.

But then He pointed to a poor old widow who dropped her last two coins in the box. The Sadducees and the rulers of the temple must have sneered at such a tiny offering. But Jesus saw it differently. "I assure you," He said, "this poor widow has given more than all the others have given. For they gave a tiny part of their surplus, but she, poor as she is, has given everything she has" (Mark 12:43–44, NLT).

The poor widow put everything she had in the offering. What a powerful statement! Do you see what Jesus is saying here? God is not interested in quantity; He is interested in quality. It means that if I give quality, then quantity will never be a problem. Advancing in the kingdom of God means giving from the heart and doing what God commands with commitment and love.

Philippians 3:12 says, "Not that I have already attained, or am already perfected..." In other words, it's not that Kingsley Fletcher has arrived. It's not that my ministry has arrived. And it's not that you have arrived, either. Don't believe for a moment that any one of us is already perfect. Rather, Paul says, "I press on, that I may lay hold of that for which Christ Jesus has also laid hold of me." That means, before the foundation of the world, Jesus Christ took hold of the kingdom, which is His rightful place to rule and reign. Then He came and took hold of you and me. Hallelujah!

Can that be true? Could God have laid hold of us before the foundations of the world? Hear what God said to the prophet Jeremiah: "Before I formed you in the womb I knew you; before you were born I sanctified you; I ordained you a prophet to the nations" (Jer. 1:5). I don't know about you, but that gets me pretty excited. It means that whatever talent we have today, God ordained it, and He prepared us to use our gifts to His glory. It means that whatever wealth or influence we may have today, God arranged it so that we could be a blessing to His kingdom. But it also means that God knows about any sorrow, pain, or disappointments you have endured. He permits suffering because it is important in His great plan for the kingdom. It's all part of the package.

Thanks to modern humanism, most of us believe that whatever we have in life is because of our talent and resourcefulness. Now, that's true to some degree. But the Word of God says that whatever we have was given to us before the world began. If we have plenty today, it's because we perfected what we had been given. If we have little today, it could be because of the environment we live in, a society ignorant of knowledge, or because God is building something in and through us that requires material sacrifice. God says, "Before I formed you in the womb I knew you. I have already called you; I have already ordained you for the ministry that I want you to pursue."

Before I was conceived in my mother's womb, I was a pastor, teacher, and missionary. It means that I was born to do what I am doing today. As Paul says, "Not that I have already attained, or am already perfected." I have not achieved what I expect to achieve in my life and ministry—there's more to come. But I am confident that God has prepared me for what I am doing now as well as for what lies ahead. I know that whatever I have accomplished is because God has prepared me for this work.

That which we are doing today we do because we are pressing on to take hold of that for which Christ Jesus took hold of us. He took hold of us so that we could lay hold of that which He prepared for us before the worlds were made. I am not satisfied to be pastor of a church of five thousand. That's just a by-product. What I have been taking hold of is beyond what the eyes can see.

THE UPWARD CALL

REGARDLESS OF PAUL'S experience as a missionary and teacher, he said that he had not yet taken hold of that which God had prepared for him. Through all the beatings, stonings, imprisonment, torture, and physical abuse he endured, Paul was convinced that he had not yet arrived. Whatever he went through, he knew that wasn't the real thing. That tells me that regardless of what we do today, it's not the real thing. If we think we've arrived, we'd better watch out. We're in for a rude awakening.

Of all the New Testament saints, there is none greater than Paul. He preached all over the world and saw hundreds, ultimately millions, come to the cross of Christ. Paul was an apostle, blinded on the road to Damascus and called to ministry by the resurrected Christ. But that ministry was not all God had for him. Paul said, "One thing I do, forgetting those things which are behind and reaching forward to those things which are ahead, I press toward the goal for the prize of the upward call of God in Christ Jesus" (Phil. 3:13–14).

Paul's prize would not be completed until he finally gave up the ghost. Regardless of what I do today, whether I receive some little rewards or see vast multitudes come to the foot of the cross, I am not supposed to be satisfied or sit back and say, "Praise God, look at what I have done!" There is yet a prize that I have been called to win. There is a prize that you were born to gain. That prize is hidden in Christ, and you will never come to it until you finally say, "I have done all I have been called to do. I have run the race; I have fought the good fight. I have completed that which I was supposed to do here on this earth."

If you truly understand the Word of God, then death will not frighten you. Today I can say that I am not afraid to die, but it took me many years to come to that point. It wasn't easy. It is only natural to be afraid of death. But Scripture tells us, "To live is Christ, and to die is gain" (Phil. 1:21). Scripture gives us a hope that is supernatural—beyond our natural fears and hopes. The Word is our strength.

No, I am not afraid to die, as long as I am sure that I have done what Christ called me to do. We cannot stop now. We are supposed to advance in the kingdom, and that means there's no time to be slack concerning God's kingdom.

Have you ever noticed that when God brings certain people out of poverty and gives them a little money, suddenly they grow arrogant and conceited? They don't want to associate with the people they used to know. They want to associate with the rich and famous. Why does that happen? Obviously they don't know the purpose for which God created them. Instead of using their wealth and blessings to bless others and to build the kingdom of God, they turn inward, rewarding themselves for their financial and social success.

Let me tell you about a young man to whom I have been ministering. He's in the energy business, and this year he will make more than five million dollars from that business. The more this country struggles with energy problems, the more money he makes. He is a very wealthy man, and the future looks very bright. But he found out that power and privilege aren't everything.

Until recently, he thought that wealth and success were the most important things in the world. He lived for money, power, and luxury. Politicians and civic leaders were coming to him, trying to persuade him to run for public office. They told him that he could be governor of the state. But he found out that he wasn't created for money. He learned that money is just a by-product of the skill that God has given him.

God has turned his life around, and he told me recently that he has accepted the call of God to go into the ministry. Today his eyes are on a very different prize—he is focused on the upward call for which Christ laid hold of him.

The Bible says that we are not to think of ourselves more highly than we should. God wants us to advance in Him. Paul says we are to forget about those things that are behind and reach forward to things ahead. Regardless of our achievement—whether it is great or small, whether we are successes or failures in this world—we are to press on toward the prize to which Christ Jesus has called us heavenward.

We live in a society that won't let people forget their mistakes. Politicians and public figures are often haunted by the sins of their youth, and so are many of us. But Paul says that if we want to obtain the prize, then we have to forget about the past. If we don't, then we won't advance in the kingdom. The Father has every reason to remember our sin and mark us as sinners. He knows us inside out, and He knows all the terrible things we have done in our lives. Yet, by the grace of God, Jesus Christ died for our sins, and God the Father has chosen to forgive us. Not because we deserve it, but because that's how much He loves us.

If God can forgive all those who call upon His name, what right do we have to hold a grudge against our brothers and sisters? If Christ can forgive our sins, then why can't we love one another and forget about the past, even though it's not easy to forget? I'm convinced that the single greatest cause of divorce is that husbands and wives won't forget the past. They keep bringing up all the bad stuff, using it as a weapon against their mates. Not only do we hold grudges against one another because of our past sins, but we even appoint ourselves as judge and jury. We convict other people in our hearts and wish evil and shame upon them.

Scripture says it so clearly: Forget about that past! That means I am not supposed to carry forward a diary of all the bad things that have happened to me. I'm not to keep a list of the wrongs I feel that someone has done to me. This is the root cause of the sin of hypocrisy.

It comes from holding onto the past. Whenever we do so, we have to live a lie. We're all smiles on the outside, but on the inside we're bottled up with hatred. We know that Christ has called us to forgive our brothers and sisters, but we're still nursing bitterness and hatred. It's eating us up.

The devil is only too happy for us to hold onto that grudge. He's thrilled when we nurse our hatred. But he's not the one we need to be concerned about. Jesus said, "Do not fear those who kill the body but cannot kill the soul. But rather fear Him who is able to destroy both soul and body in hell" (Matt. 10:28). Let me paraphrase that verse: "Don't trouble yourself over what men can do to you. Don't fret about the wiles of the devil. Don't make plans based on what may or may not happen to your physical body; rather, remember what God has said and focus your life and thoughts on the principles of the kingdom." Jesus said, "Let the dead bury their own dead, but you go and preach the kingdom of God" (Luke 9:60). In other words, forget the past and get on with life.

BUILDING MORE BARNS

IN LUKE 12, Jesus tells the story of a certain rich man whose harvest was so plentiful and the land produced such a good crop that he worried, "What am I going to do? I have no place to store my crops." He worried about it for a time, then he said, "Aha, I know! I'll tear down my old barns and build bigger ones!" He was so proud of himself that he said, "Why, I'll have everything I need for the rest of my life! Then I can take it easy—eat, drink, and be merry!" But before he could even finish the sentence, God said, "You fool! You won't survive this night, and you'll soon lose everything you have."

No one denied that the man had worked hard for his good fortune. He planned ahead, built good barns, and was so successful that his harvest was tremendous. He did what any good farmer should do, and he achieved his success the old-fashioned way—he earned it! But the Scriptures say that in his moment of arrogance, pride, and self-flattery, he blew it. Why? Because he was not looking to God for his reward.

He wasn't seeking the kingdom of God and His righteousness; he personified the words of a song by Frank Sinatra. He thumped his chest and said, "Look at me! I did it MY way!" A fool is someone who makes decisions based on his own rationale without considering what God would have him do. The wisdom of the kingdom does not reason with the heart. Kingdom wisdom reasons by the Word of God and the guidance of the Holy Spirit.

Do you see what the foolish man did? He didn't consult the Lord and ask, "Father, what shall I do about my bountiful harvest?" He didn't put the past behind him and forget about his successes. He said, "Man, look what I've done! I'm fixed for life. I'm such a great farmer, everything I planned is paying off now, and I can eat, drink, and be merry!"

This man was saying, "I'm just going to retire. I'm going to take it easy!" As I studied this passage, I became convinced that it is wrong for believers to retire. Retirement is *not* part of God's plan for us. Retire from what? People who retire tend to get sick more easily than those who continue fully occupied. They get arthritis, heart problems, suffer from stress, and experience more physical and emotional difficulties than those who feel they are still useful and productive in life. The mortality rate of newly retired people is incredibly high. I think that's part of what Jesus is talking about in this parable.

If we are serious about our relationship with God, we won't linger on the past, and we won't go around patting ourselves on the back because we've had good fortune. The Bible says, "For promotion cometh neither from the east, nor from the west, nor from the south. But God is the judge: he putteth down one, and setteth up another" (Ps. 75:6–7, KJV). This man, however, said, "When I get those new barns, I'm just going to lay back and enjoy all I've achieved. I am going to take life easy—lots of eating, lots of drinking, and I am really going to party!"

I imagine he planned to visit all his grandchildren; maybe he planned to get a Winnebago motor home and travel to all the national parks. He just wanted to have a good time. But God said, "You fool! This very night your life will be taken from you; then who will get what you have prepared for yourself?"

This is how it will be for everyone who stores up treasures for himself but ignores the things of God. This is what can happen to anyone who stores up for himself and gives no thought to the needs of others. What have you given to God lately? Have you been hoarding your treasure, planning that great day when you can retire and run away to some beautiful place and congratulate yourself for your thrift and wise planning?

Thank God for the things we are able to store up to provide for our future needs, but please be careful that you don't act like this unfortunate man. God knows if our motives are wrong. Instead of forgetting the past and asking the Lord's guidance for what to do next, the rich man was more interested in his own pleasures; he totally ignored what he knew to be right.

I believe that one reason so many churches are dead today is because they grow to a certain point, they begin to look around and observe how prosperous they've become, and they quit doing what God created them to do—to win lives to Christ. Instead of reaching out to the lost, growing in grace and knowledge, touching the lives of families, helping the needy, blessing the hungry and the needy, and conducting ministries that allow them to fulfill their calling, they start spending all their time planning dinners, banquets, picnics, festivals, and concerts—celebrating the harvest.

When the church starts congratulating herself for her achievements and taking more pleasure in her success than in ministering to those in need, then she has deserted her true calling and has quit doing what she was designed to do. No longer are we focused on what God desires or what God can do, but on what we can accomplish through our own wisdom, long-range planning, and human ingenuity. We're just laying up treasures and building more barns.

One day the Spirit of God will speak, and He will say, "You fools! You have stored all these things for yourselves and not for me!" Look at this warning very carefully. God expects us to advance in His kingdom, not to sit back and enjoy what we've attained. If we've been blessed as a church, we won't have to beg for money. God will meet our needs. If we've been blessed with creative and committed leaders, we won't have to wrack our brains for new programs. God will open the doors.

The day that I go into the pulpit in my home church and start begging for money is the day I will know that I have missed God somewhere.

This is not to say that the church can't appreciate what God has accomplished in her midst, and it's not to say that we shouldn't be pleased when we see that our plans and programs are working and souls are being saved. But be cautious. We have the all-too-human temptation to kick back and take it easy, to spend money that God has provided in ways that make sense to us without concern for what God intended, or to just have fun when we need to be working. It's a temptation we have to resist, because that kind of thinking has weakened many churches and stopped the Spirit of God from flowing in their midst. Trust me: If we retire as a church, God will stop blessing us.

We must remember that it is God who gives promotion. When we begin to think that we've done something on our own and start patting ourselves on the back—either as a church or as individual believers—we are in great danger. The Lord says to those who resist His authority, "You hypocrite! You come to church on Sunday and tell Me that you love Me, but then you do it your way and make your own plans without My counsel." Before long, we're more interested in the world's values than the Word of God. We claim to love God, but before long we're finding fault with the people of God.

How much do we really love God? Do we love Him enough to give our last ounce of strength to serve Him? Will we serve Him with every breath we breathe, without seeking after our own pleasures? To what extent will we serve Him? If we really love someone, we can't fake it. It shows all over our face. We want to spend time with the one we love. When we're with that special someone, we completely lose track of time. Is that how we feel in the presence of God? Is that how we feel in the house of God? We say that we love Him, but do we really? Or are we becoming more like this man who loved Him in word only, whose heart was far from God?

BE FAITHFUL IN ALL THINGS

GOD IS CALLING us to advance in His kingdom. Do you know what *promotion* means? It means "increased responsibility." It is not a reward. It is not a trophy that you get because you're such a great person. It is the recognition of your ability to work a little harder and do a little more.

Unfortunately, we don't all receive promotions. One reason is because there are a lot of lazy people in our churches. These are the people who became Christians to escape hell. They're not interested in advancing in the kingdom of God; they're just happy to be there. But God has a warning for the believer who feels that way: "Because you are lukewarm, and neither cold nor hot, I will vomit you out of My mouth" (Rev. 3:16).

He is saying, "I will throw them out of My kingdom." Oh, yes, lazy people can come up with a lot of excuses. But the end result is always the same: They never do anything. The moment I become lazy, I am inviting the spirit of poverty into my life. There is no place for laziness and apathy in the church of Jesus Christ. If we lose our drive and our enthusiasm to serve God, we will not be able to do the things God has commissioned us to do.

When we look around at many of the mainline denominations today we see apathy, division, and apostasy. But they didn't start out that way. They got that way because one day they looked around and noticed that they were becoming successful and wealthy; they decided they needed to build more barns to store all their resources. Some study or census report somewhere confirmed that they were among the largest denominations in the world, and they started to relax.

Let me go a step further. The Charismatic movement didn't start out the way it is today, either. Sometime during the seventies or early eighties it looked around and saw that it was part of something big, and it was growing even bigger. Suddenly it realized it was a movement, and it was growing bigger, getting richer, accumulating more and more property, and attracting lots of new members. Its members were tempted to compare sizes and numbers, rather than looking for fruitfulness and fulfillment.

I am saddened when I see what is taking place in some of our churches today. We have grown so fast that many congregations and denominations are in danger of becoming complacent in their ministry and work. They practice what we call high-class, sophisticated religious politics. That's why the growth has suddenly stopped. When they desert the true calling of Christ, there is no blessing. If we want God to bless us, we have to be effective. We can't sit back and retire! We must get back to what made us strong and come back to the conviction and spirit of the full gospel.

Jesus Christ, the righteous Lamb of God, is saying to today's church, "Nevertheless I have this against you, that you have left your first love." He is saying to every congregation, every minister of the gospel, and every true believer, "Remember therefore from where you have fallen; repent and do the first works, or else I will come to you quickly and remove your lampstand from its place—unless you repent" (Rev. 2:4–5). Do you hear His voice, my brothers and sisters? Then I call upon you to return to your first love.

Serving ourselves instead of the God who loves us is sheer folly. The Bible says that if we know how to do something and we don't do it, it is sin. If we know we're supposed to do something to serve God, but instead we're sitting back and relaxing, it is sin. Laziness is a curse. Now you may wish I wouldn't say these things, but I cannot deny the conviction of the Holy Spirit. Truth sets people free, and I am obligated to preach that truth. The day that I come to church afraid to speak the truth is the day I will be disqualified to serve the Lord. If I ever write a word that compromises what God has called me to declare, then I will have betrayed my calling. I have to speak the word as God lays it upon my heart.

Promotion does not come because someone likes us; it comes because we have shown ourselves faithful, trustworthy, hardworking, and reliable. We can be counted on to keep our promises and fulfill our obligations. Therefore, we've shown that we're ready for the next step. That's what it means to advance. We can't expect promotion until we show that we've been able to handle what God has given us.

I believe that one reason many people are having so many problems is because they have succumbed to the spirit of laziness. They dream of driving fine cars, living in lovely homes, and marrying the most attractive woman or man. But they're not willing to work hard to get those things. That attitude has hurt many people.

I Have Seen the Kingdom

Do you want a better job? What did you do in your last job to prove that you're worthy of a better one? Have you been a faithful, loyal, capable, and hard-working employee? What quality is your work? What have you done in your church to show that you deserve greater responsibility? Do you want an increase in salary? What have you done in your present position to prove that you're worthy of a raise?

My brother and sister, hear these words of Jesus in the parable of the unrighteous servant: "He who is faithful in what is least is faithful also in much; and he who is unjust in what is least is unjust also in much. Therefore if you have not been faithful in the unrighteous mammon, who will commit to your trust the true riches?" (Luke 16:10–11).

Do you want to advance in the kingdom of God? Then be faithful in all you do; show that you are worthy of promotion. Are you faithful on the job, in the home, in the community, and in your church? It all matters, you know. Faithful people are faithful in all things.

God revealed something to me several years ago. He said, "Never give anybody anything until that person has shown by his actions that he's qualified by need, example, character, faithfulness, and training." As you seek promotion from God, God asks, "Are you qualified?" Yes, you may have all the dreams in the world, but He's asking, "Are you qualified?" If God has given you responsibilities in one area of life, then He will be watching carefully to see how you conduct yourself in that area first. Believe me, He will not promote you to greater things until you've proven that you can be trusted with lesser things.

If you are an usher in the church, then do the job faithfully. Be a good usher. Be faithful, be on time, be courteous, and be helpful. Be there. If you're in the choir, then sing faithfully and be there, on time, when you're needed. Listen to instruction. Sing as unto the Lord. If you can be trusted with little things, imagine how exciting it's going to be when God reveals that He is ready to trust you with bigger ones!

Quality is needed in the church just as it is needed in industry. It's very important. Too often, Christians think of church commitments more as hobbies. Church commitments are just something we do on weekends or in the evening when we're not doing anything more important. Church is like a country club where we go and see people we know. Our kids go to Sunday school, we put a little money in the plate, we join a committee or a Bible study, and we think God ought to be grateful for all we're doing. We feel as if we're doing God a big favor. If that's your attitude, don't be surprised if God withholds your next promotion.

BEING FAITHFUL IN MUCH

GOD EXPECTS QUALITY from us. "If you are going to serve Me," He says, "then make sure you do it with quality." Whatever we do, we have to make sure we serve our heavenly Father with real dedication and commitment. God will only promote us when He sees that we are qualified and are committed. We can't go to stage two in life or ministry until we've been proven faithful in the lesser things.

I have prayed, "God, don't give us any more souls until we are able to care for the ones we have." I've even said, "God, don't give us any new buildings or facilities until we've shown that we're faithful in the ones we have." Maybe more of us should use this approach in our family lives. Do we want a victorious marriage? Then put some quality into it. God is the one who promotes. If we put quality into whatever we do, God will promote. As I travel across this nation and around the world, I realize that we have a duty as people of God to rededicate ourselves to the idea of quality in our lives and ministries.

In another parable in Luke 16, Jesus tells about the manager who was accused of wasting his master's possessions. The rich man called in his servant and asked him, "What's this I hear about you?" You see, the master had given his manager responsibility over all his accounts, but the man had abused his privileges. So the boss said, "Give an account of yourself, because you can no longer be my manager."

The manager thought to himself, *What am I going to do now? My master is taking away my job. I'm not strong enough to do common labor, and I'm too proud to beg. What can I do?*

After he thought about it, he said, "I know what I'll do: If I'm going to lose my job, then I'll fix it so that other people will welcome me into their houses." He called each of his master's debtors and asked, "How much do you owe my master?" The first owed a hundred gallons of oil. The manager said, "Sit down here. Take your bill, quickly, and make it fifty gallons." He asked each debtor how much was owed; each time he had them reduce their debt.

What do you think the master said about what his manager had done? Do you think he had him beaten? No, not at all. He praised the man because he had acted so shrewdly! The word *shrewd* has two meanings. First, it means "cunning, deceptive." But it also means "smart, crafty, clever." In the parable, the master actually compliments this crafty manager because he was so smart.

If you have a job to do and you can't do it, wouldn't it be wise to get someone else to do it for you? The manager in the parable knew that he needed people to help him after he had lost his job, so he took this shrewd approach; it was the surest way to provide for his own future.

You might think that Jesus would have been critical of this type of behavior. After all, the manager was being dishonest. But Jesus was making another point: If the people of this world are shrewd and clever in their dealings and financial matters, then people of the light need to be just as clever in doing the work of the kingdom.

Too often, unbelievers are smarter in their own ways than believers are in theirs. When godless and profane people of this world go to their jobs, they follow their employer's instructions and do what the boss says. They don't make up excuses or get angry because they don't get the credit they deserve. Most believers could learn a few things from the secular world. When the man on the street does his job, he generally does it right, because if he doesn't he'll be fired. How sad to realize that those without God, living in the kingdom of this world, are often wiser and shrewder than those of God's kingdom. They are advancing, but we are falling behind.

When it comes to laying up treasures, the people of the world are smarter than we are. Jesus says, "I say to you, make friends for yourselves by unrighteous mammon, that when you fail, they may receive you into an everlasting home." That's when He says, "He who is faithful in what is least is faithful also in much; and he who is unjust in what is least is unjust also in much" (Luke 16:9–10).

But what does the church say? "Run away from them! We're so religious that we don't want to learn anything from unsaved people." Consequently, we don't reach the lost, and we don't have access to the skills that new believers can bring to the church. God wants people to be accountable. He expects us to be faithful in our tasks.

I have been sent to help, and I have been sent to teach. The Lord is asking me to display excellence in my ministry—not to make excuses and not to accept them either. We can't accept sloppy performance simply because believers are often seen as second-class citizens in the eyes of the world.

We don't have to go it alone. The Holy Spirit says, "If that is what God is calling you to do, then I will go along beside you and help you do it." But the Holy Spirit will not do the job. He comes to give us the strength to fulfill our calling. He is the Comforter, the Helper, the *Paraclete,* which means "the one who comes alongside." He is not our Holy Fix-it Man! If we want to advance in the kingdom, then we need to know how to do "our utmost for His highest," with the Holy Spirit as our Comforter and Guide, not our temporary replacement.

Jesus goes on to say, "Use worldly wealth to gain friends for yourselves so that when it's gone, you will be welcomed into eternal dwellings." We are not to stay on our little islands and make ourselves into pious recluses; we are to get involved with the people of this world. There are things we can learn from them. They don't sit around waiting on someone else to do their job for them; they do it, and they keep on going.

Jesus says that before you can be trusted with bigger things, first you've got to prove yourself reliable with the very little things. If you have not been trustworthy with someone else's property, why would God allow you to gain property of your own?

A TIME OF TESTING

AS WE HAVE seen, the environment in the church today doesn't teach us much about the nature of life in the kingdom. That's why we have to make a conscious effort to learn about it and to discover God's purpose for the church today. One thing we need to know is that God does not intend for us to be dependent on others, and He doesn't expect us to be independent either. He wants us to be *inter-dependent*. He expects us to depend, first of all, on Him, and second of all, on one another.

I've known some believers with a bad case of the "gimmes." They've been taught that God's job is to give them everything they want. "God, give me this, and God, give me that." But when the "gimmes" don't provide all the stuff to which they think they're entitled, they start running around looking for some new seminar or self-help book or some popular quick-fix artist to tell them how to get back on God's gravy train.

We don't have to look far in the evangelical world today to see all the spiritual fitness coaches out there with their seminars, books, and tapes, trying to show a generation of acquisitive believers how to squeeze more goodies out of God. When we try to approach God on that basis, however, we set ourselves up for a big letdown. And if we try to live the Christian life with the democratic spirit of independence, we have it exactly backward.

I also have a word for those believers who come to the house of God just to get their fire insurance. If you only joined the church to escape the risk of hellfire, God has a surprise for you. Not everyone who says, "Lord, Lord," will enter the kingdom of heaven—only those who do the will of the Father in heaven. The church isn't a fire escape; it's a way of life.

If you're only in it for the goodies you can get out of God, you're going to be very disappointed. The mark of Christian maturity is not how much you can get, but how much you can give. If you really want blessings, you need to be the giver. Jesus said, "It is more blessed to give than to receive" (Acts 20:35). If you understand the spirit of giving, serving one another will not be a problem for you. It's the mark of greatness in God's kingdom.

Many who lived in the province of Judea two thousand years ago thought Jesus of Nazareth was a little strange at times. He did things they didn't understand. They saw that He spoke as one with authority—more like a king than a humble carpenter. But even His brothers didn't get it at first. They didn't believe in Him. But Jesus said, "My time has not yet come, but your time is always ready" (John 7:5–6). "The world isn't going to hate you," He said, "but it will hate Me because I have come to testify against this world system and to reveal its corruption."

Jesus wasn't interested in pleasing people with His words. More often than not, His words were painful and embarrassing. He tested and probed the people, especially the pious religious people, thus revealing what they were made of. He tested them mainly to make them come face to face with the difficult questions He raised in His teaching. He wanted each one to come to grips with the truth.

He asked the disciples, "Who do men say that I am?" He knew the answer, but He wanted them to think about His true identity for themselves. When He preached the Sermon on the Mount, He said, "Philip, where can we buy bread to feed all these people?" Again, He knew the answer. The very next verse says, "He was testing Philip, for he already knew what he was going to do" (John 6:5–6, TLB). He asked because He wanted Philip and the disciples to come to grips with the fact that only the true Son of God could provide a meal for so many people under the circumstances.

Right now, Jesus is asking you: "What will you do with the gifts I have given you?" He is waiting for your response. Is He asking because He doesn't know what you will decide? Or is He, in fact, asking because He wants to provoke you to deal with your own role in the church and to provoke you to come to grips with the truths that He is showing you in His Word?

Our great King will not allow anyone who has started maturing in the faith to live like a baby on a diet of milk. He won't allow us to continue indefinitely as mere babes in the Word. He expects us to grow, to multiply, and to advance in the kingdom. He demands that we grow in the grace and knowledge of our Lord and Savior Jesus Christ, so that He might be glorified in His kingdom. Is that your hope today? Do you live for the glory of God? Are you seeking His kingdom and His righteousness so that He may one day lavish His abundance upon you? I trust that you are. It's the only treasure that really matters.

On the other hand, Christ will not allow you to give your loyalty to any other kingdom that competes with His. If you allow the world's values to control your thoughts, you will end up by default in the world of humanism and apostasy that is such an affront to our Lord. So desire to grow in faith, to advance, and to seek the kingdom of our Lord, rejecting every false kingdom and every competing domain.

It is my prayer that no man or woman who reads these words will ever be idle, complacent, or passive in his or her walk of faith. Jesus warns that if we try to sit back and relax, He will remove His lampstand from the church. He also says He will vomit us out of His mouth. If we try to sit on the fence with one foot in the kingdom of God and the other in the kingdoms of this world, the Scripture warns that we will be cast into outer darkness. But if we reject the impostors and demonstrate by our labor and example that we value the prize that Christ has laid up for us in His kingdom, then one day we will gain the greatest treasure of all.

Will you focus your thoughts and prayers on Him today? Will you make His kingdom and His righteousness your passionate pursuit? I pray that you will. For it is only when Jesus Christ is your heart's deep desire that you can advance in His kingdom.

7

Exalting the King

WHEN YOU'RE IN love with someone, there will be times when you are overcome by emotion. If you're truly in love, the object of your affections will be on your mind night and day. Whenever you have to part, your heart will ache to be near the one you love again. If you should catch a glimpse of him or her from a distance, your heart leaps and your blood pressure soars. When you're deeply in love, there will be times when your spirit just overflows with delight, and tears of joy will roll down your cheeks. That's how people commonly express their feelings for those they love deeply.

Does that describe your emotions for the God who created you, who loves you with an everlasting love, who gave the life of His only begotten Son to redeem you? Is that how you feel when you come into the house of God? When you're away, on the job, or traveling somewhere, do you ache to be in His presence once again, to spend time with the Father in prayer, to sing praises to His name in the sanctuary? Is it your heart's desire to praise and worship the King, to glorify Him, to be close to Him, to feel His touch, and to hear His gentle voice speaking to you through the Word of God?

Some of us—actually, I fear, most of us—have never felt that kind of emotion for our heavenly Father. If we praise and worship God as we should, we will never have a dry face. But, I'm sorry to say, most of us worship with dry faces—faces like flint—because we don't know what it means to worship and glorify the King. We feel

121

more emotion for actors and actresses on television or on the big screen than for our Maker. We feel more devotion to our family pets than to our Creator. We go through the motions of prayer and praise, on Sunday we sing hymns and recite words that we learned years ago, but the idea that we should weep and rejoice in the presence of our King and declare our undying devotion to Him is, frankly, inconceivable to many believers today.

Our minds are so full of worries. We're preoccupied with our own needs, hopes, plans, amusements, or appetites for our next meal, and we let those things rob the glory from God. But if you steal God's glory, you don't have very much to give Him in praise. That's why so many people don't know how to praise God; they've been stealing His glory. Instead of focusing their attention on God, they focus inwardly on themselves.

True worship is adoration, reverence, and devotion to the object of our affections. When I sing His praises, I'm not focusing on myself, on my singing, or on my own efforts. If I'm singing for the glory of God, I forget myself. I'm merely an instrument of praise. In fact, it's not even me who sings, but the Spirit of God sings through me. Instead of trying to prove how devout I am, I focus on how great He is and give Him all the glory. We are to worship the King.

The kind of attitude and emotion we should have when we come into the presence of our King is illustrated in the well-known song, "O Worship the King." This great hymn was composed in 1815 by Robert Grant, using a melody that was composed by Johann M. Haydn. The ancient words radiate the image of a mighty King— "pavilioned in splendor, and girded with praise." It says the canopy of His royal pavilion is the heavens. The dome of His cathedral is the universe beyond. This is not the vulgar image of God that the world wants to give you, that of some angry scorekeeper up in the sky. This is a portrait of a loving, caring, heavenly Father who is our shield and defender. It's a picture of One in whom we can put our trust, knowing His love will never fail. His mercies are tender and firm to the end. He is our God and Father; He is our Maker, Defender, Redeemer, and Friend. This is why we praise His name!

I can't help it if tears roll down my cheeks when I stand before my King. I'm not ashamed to weep in His presence. Weeping is not a sign of my weakness. I weep because my God is so strong, so majestic, so loving, and so worthy of praise. I praise Him because I know Him. I weep because I love Him. I glorify Him because I know from whence I've come. When I first came to this country, I slept on the bare floor of my small apartment near the campus of the University of North Carolina. But I never worried, because I knew that God was with me then, just as He is with me now. Whom should I fear?

When I come into His presence, I think of His wondrous works to the children of men. How can I express what's in my heart? Mere words cannot describe His greatness. I cry out to Him, "Oh, Father, tell me how to praise You!" I lift my voice to Him. I worship Him. With the prophet Isaiah I cry out, "Surely God is my salvation; I will trust and not be afraid. The LORD, the LORD, is my strength and my song; he has become my salvation" (Isa. 12:2, NIV). Can you hear it now? Surely it is God who saves me; I will trust in Him and not be afraid. For the Lord is my stronghold and my sure defense, and He will be my Savior!

When I don't know how to praise God, the Spirit speaks to me, saying, "Let Me tell you what the Father desires to hear." And the gentle voice of God's love sings through me. The Spirit helps me when I don't know what to say. He perfects the words of my mouth. Paul says, "Likewise the Spirit also helps in our weaknesses. For we do not know what we should pray for as we ought, but the Spirit Himself makes intercession for us with groanings which cannot be uttered." The Holy Spirit knows what the Father wishes to hear. Paul goes on to say, "He who searches the hearts knows what the mind of the Spirit is, because He makes intercession for the saints according to the will of God" (Rom. 8:26–27).

We may pray boldly and worship with confidence, because our praise is perfected in Him. David sings, "O LORD, our Lord, how excellent is Your name in all the earth, who have set Your glory above the heavens! Out of the mouth of babes and nursing infants You have ordained strength" (Ps. 8:1–2). When our words come to the ears of a holy and righteous God, He hears perfect prayer and praise. The Holy Spirit speaks them perfectly on our behalf. But how tragic it is when some of us refuse to cooperate with the Holy

Spirit. How sad it is when we allow the secular baggage of this world to interfere with our act of worship or when we let religious traditions and doctrinal disputes block our adoration. Sometimes we are more like actors with attitudes than worshipers.

When we understand who God is and how His kingdom operates, we will want to exalt and magnify our King. When we come into His presence, we will know that there are angels all around us who glorify His name day and night. Where we stand in the house of God is holy ground, the rightful domain of the living God. When the angels of the Lord encamp around about us, our attitudes must change. We will tell our children, "Listen, child! Listen! We are in the presence of the King. Be on your best behavior." For the house of God is holy ground.

Let me say something else. When we come into the presence of a king, we never come empty-handed. We come with gifts. We bring him the most precious offerings we can give. Some of us come empty-handed into the house of God because we don't know the protocol of the kingdom. The gifts we bring to Him are not because our King is poor or because He needs what we have. No, it's because the kingdom provides comfort, peace, and blessings to its subjects. When we bring Him gifts, we are telling the King that we love Him and appreciate His bountiful provision. We are expressing our gratitude.

When Jesus Christ was born in Bethlehem of Judea, the Magi came looking for Him. They came in caravans from the kingdoms of the East, bearing gifts of gold, frankincense, and myrrh. Why such elaborate and costly gifts for a mere infant? What on earth would a child do with such extravagant presents? Ah, that's where you miss the point. The point is not that the recipient needs or wants the gifts—in kingdom protocol, the value of the gift demonstrates the level of esteem that the giver holds for the king. Do we still feel that way toward our King? Not really. I've said it before: We are the only people who steal from our King by holding back on our tithes and offerings. We must not do that.

Some of us are quite content for our King to be poor. We give Him so little. Yet, we expect Him to bless us with great bounty. We're upset if He doesn't give us nice homes, comfortable cars, big-screen TVs, and an outdoor spa! But we don't care if the house of God is barren. True worshipers will worship the King in spirit and in truth—that's what the Bible says. They will be the ones who come to God with their tithes and offerings. When they enter into the presence of the Lord, they will not come empty-handed. They understand that God wants to see how honest they are and how much they appreciate the protection and favors that He has provided.

The kingdom of God has come, and the power of God is working in our midst. The principles of the kingdom are working for us. When I came to America I was like the seventy evangelists in Luke 10, with neither moneybag, knapsack, nor sandals. But I knew that I did not have to worry; my Father is faithful. When I say that I will never lack for anything, I'm not saying it because I have such an abundance. It's because my Father is a great King, and He provides for me. When I come to the house of God, I don't come as a big shot; I come in brokenness. But I come with peace and joy because I know that in the house of God I have access to the throne room of heaven.

HONORING THE FATHER

LET ME TELL you a secret I learned as a very small boy in my father's household in Africa. As long as the king is sitting on the throne, you must address him as king. But when he's off the throne, he is Daddy. Whenever you present your requests and bring your case, you must speak to the king with dignity and honor. In public or on any formal occasion, you must address him as "Your Majesty," "Your Highness," or "Sir." When you bring your gift to him, you will never put it directly into his hands, but you will give it to his servants first; they will give it to the king when the time is right.

Whatever you bring to our great King is holy unto God. In fact, the moment you say it is for the King, it becomes holy; the King will receive that which you have given Him. If the King knows that what you've given Him is all that you have, He will call His ministers together and say, "Look, he has given Me all he has. He is giving out of need. He is My devoted servant." Anytime you come to Him, He will say, "Make sure his needs are met."

125

I Have Seen the Kingdom

When you come before a king, you never come with an attitude. You come in humility. When you humble yourself before him, he has the opportunity of exalting you. In so doing, he accepts you and confers honor upon you. He takes you from your lowly position and lifts you up. God is looking for a people who will come to Him in humility so He can lift them up. The Bible says, "Therefore humble yourselves under the mighty hand of God, that He may exalt you in due time" (1 Pet. 5:6).

Where are the men and women who will exalt the King of kings and praise His name in the sanctuary? Where are the subjects of the King who will lift up His name and glorify Him before all men? God is looking for such people. Peter says, "For the eyes of the LORD are on the righteous, and His ears are open to their prayers; but the face of the LORD is against those who do evil" (1 Pet. 3:12). And the authors of the Book of 2 Chronicles tell us, "For the eyes of the LORD run to and fro throughout the whole earth, to show Himself strong on behalf of those whose heart is loyal to Him" (2 Chron. 16:9).

When you delight the heart of the King, He is inclined to hear your petitions and to grant your requests. Many times, however, when we come before the King to make our requests, we come in dragging, hanging our heads, sorrowful and downcast, and wondering why He is not eager to hear our prayers. If you want to get the King's attention, praise Him. Exalt His name and glorify Him, and He will hear your prayers. To get practical and useful gifts from Him, please Him with your devotion and sincere, childlike petitions. You say you are a child of the King, but if you come into His presence looking more like a broken thing—downcast, dejected, and miserable—how will He even recognize you as His child? The child of a King should be joyful and full of vitality!

In the kingdom of God we are all royalty. King's kids don't beg. Whatever the King possesses belongs to us already, because we are heirs of the King. We should sing His praises and declare His works glorious. Peter declares, "But you are a chosen generation, a royal priesthood, a holy nation, His own special people, that you may proclaim the praises of Him who called you out of darkness into His marvelous light" (1 Pet. 2:9). Once you were not a people, but now you are the people of God. You were once outside the realm of

God's mercy; but now you have received mercy.

It is always a joy to come into the King's chambers. The children of the King have special privileges. They know the King in a very special way, and they may be ushered into the presence of the King even when others are kept waiting. This is our privilege as children of God.

As I travel around this country, I occasionally meet people who grew up in poverty. They had difficult lives. But they had a valuable talent, or they worked very hard, or somehow or other they managed to come into a great deal of money. Suddenly they are people of wealth and position. The wealth went straight to their heads.

They forgot where they came from, and they don't want to associate with the people they used to know. They don't want to talk like they did when they were living in poverty. I have even seen some of them trying to put on an accent like mine, with a touch of Africa! They want to look, sound, act, and think like somebody else. They're ashamed of who they are.

Jesus says we are not to be concerned about what we're going to eat, what we're going to drink, or what we have to wear. Our heavenly Father already knows all of our needs. But whatever we have, He says, "Bring it to Me. Come to Me. I don't need what you have, but I want to see how willing you are to give up your treasure for Me. I gave you what you have, and I am the only one who can meet your needs in this life. Your treasure will not save you, but you can demonstrate your love for Me by your willingness to use what I've given you for the glory of My kingdom."

We have the mentality that the harder we work and the more material possessions we have, the more other people should be impressed by us. We think we are successful in the eyes of the world. But God looks at that success as pride and arrogance, and He says, "No, My dear child. I gave you what you have. Your wealth is for your use, but I also expect you to use a portion of your treasure for building My kingdom."

After the Crucifixion, Jesus needed a tomb in which to be buried. A rich man named Joseph of Arimathea came forward and supplied His need. Why did Joseph do that? After all, his world did not hold Jesus of Nazareth in very high regard. They scorned Him, humiliated Him, cursed Him, and crucified Him. Jesus proclaimed a message that was contrary to the teachings of the Pharisees and the Sadducees.

But this man had been converted, and he realized that whatever he had was God's property first. He gave unto God unselfishly, and his act of generosity is remembered to this very day. If you have a car, it belongs to God. If you have a house, it belongs to God. If you have children, they also belong to God. If you have a business, that business belongs to God. Whatever you have is His. But the man who pulls himself up by his own bootstraps is more likely to say to himself, "My goodness, look at all the things I have done! Why, I can relax now and begin to enjoy all the wealth I've accumulated!"

But God says, "Excuse Me! Wait just a minute, My friend. What do you plan to do with all this treasure when you're dead?"

A MINISTRY OF LOVE

IF WE CLING to our treasure, our motives are wrong. We are trying to keep everything for ourselves. We only want people to see how rich we are. If we're believers, then whatever we have is from the Lord. When I came to America, I left everything behind; I slept on the floor of my small apartment for three months. There were moments when I wondered why God would allow me to go through all this. But now I believe that God was checking me out. He wanted to see if He could trust me with something bigger. Early on He trained me to know that whatever I have is of Him. My heart could rejoice, but I had to keep my head out of it.

If I were to boast about my spiritual battle scars, I could probably make you feel sorry for me. But today I count all those things as blessings and as a preparation for the work that Christ had prepared for me to do. Advancing in the kingdom, I discovered that I could not sit back and wait on some supernatural blessing to come to me in the great by and by. God never gave me the time to relax and retire. I had an appointment, with my name on it, set by the Department of Eternal Affairs, which was the ministry of the gospel.

When I accepted my position with that department, I agreed to do any job the Boss gave me to do, no questions asked. So I began, and I worked my way up, never seeking any particular position but doing whatever I found to do for which I was qualified.

At times I wish people could see the way I grew up as a boy, back in my native village, going barefoot through the bush, with cuts all over me. It was often difficult, but does that mean I've paid my dues?

It is not that I was so poor. I did come from a royal home, but I learned that I had to work hard for any success I expected to have in life. I knew the parable of the rich man, and I wasn't going to let any of those things go to my head. But once God began to speak to my heart, I set out with a sense of mission. I knew that God had a plan for me and that I was going to be in the ministry. In August 1966 I took my office in the Department of Eternal Affairs.

If you do a shabby job, don't expect God to reward your labors. And don't try to over-spiritualize your job—just do what you're paid to do. If I work for you it is my responsibility to do that work with the best intent at heart and to do the best job I know how to do. My work should always be "as unto the Lord." My attitude in whatever task I undertake will show whether or not I am ready for promotion.

Too often, we believers have a sloppy attitude. Most of us are not qualified to move in the gifts of the Spirit. We are supposed to love the Lord with all our hearts. Too often, however, we love Him only with our lips. God says, "I am looking for someone who will stand in the gap." But how can we stand in the gap if we are spiritually lazy?

God searches the heart, and He sees if there is any wickedness there. If there is any compartment in our hearts where wrong motives survive, He will discover it. That's why David prayed, "Search me, O God, and know my heart; try me, and know my anxieties; and see if there is any wicked way in me, and lead me in the way everlasting" (Ps. 139:23–24).

We need to allow the Holy Spirit to probe our hearts and minds, showing us those areas where sin lingers. He must reveal to us every sin that we have not yet confessed. In order to advance in the kingdom of God, there are some things that we have to do. No longer are we going to say, "Holy Ghost, You do it!" The Holy

Spirit is there to assist—not to do the job. He knows how to deliver from temptation. He knows how to care for those who serve Him faithfully. He says, "As long as you are submitted completely to Me, I will exalt you. As long as you humble yourself before My throne, I will honor you. As long as you give unto Me, I will make sure that you get back whatever you need."

That is God's principle. If we cannot be trusted in small things, then God says we are not qualified to handle the greater things He has in mind. When we honor God, He will always find a way to bless us in return. But if we neglect our worship of Him, if we fail to exalt His name, and if we shortchange Him, we are hurting ourselves most of all.

God would not be the wise God that He is if He made us what we were not qualified to be. Anyone who holds high office, whether it is the White House, the Congress, or any other position of leadership, is expected to be trustworthy and honest. If God puts someone into a position of trust and he or she is dishonest, then part of the discredit will fall on God. Now, I believe that there are times when He allows some corrupt leaders to rise because the fall from power can be a judgment or perhaps a lesson for them. But in most cases God honors those whose hearts are pure and whose integrity stands in Him.

Why do you suppose we have so few believers in high government offices these days? Why are so few of the civic and cultural leaders in this society people of faith? Could it be that most believers are not qualified to handle the demands of such offices? Think about it. Believers have a dangerous tendency of running away from reality. Instead of facing challenging situations, we prefer to deny that there's a problem, and we trust someone else to deal with it. The church needs to handle her own problems.

For example, I hear people calling for Bible reading in the schools. But I'm convinced that if our children were reading the Bible at home and in the church, we wouldn't have to worry about what they're reading at school. The school teacher doesn't raise our children—we do. If the government says that there's to be no Bible reading in school, why not take responsibility for reading the Bible to our children at home?

A MINISTRY OF RECONCILIATION

IF CHRISTIANS ACTUALLY started living out daily what we claim to believe on Sundays, we would change the world. There wouldn't be any culture wars. Society would be crying out for the principles of our faith, because they would see the power of God demonstrated in our daily lives. If we really want to make changes in this nation, we need to take the bull by the horns and face these issues with the conviction that God is greater than our problems.

God gives to each one according to his or her abilities. Tragically, most of us are not qualified to be blessed by God. We want to advance in the kingdom of God, but we have made the kingdom the lowest priority in our lives. We say, "Let me do it my way!" But we need to learn to do it God's way. We want a promotion. We pray for it, we jockey to get it, and then when we get it we say, "Look what I've done!" Our pride disqualifies us for real service.

We need to make sure that we don't get ahead of God. When we push God out of the picture, we're all alone; we will soon find ourselves growing weaker and less productive.

We can't expect good things to come if we don't have the right attitude. God is the source of all good gifts, and He expects us to multiply whatever we've received from Him. We're not to hide our treasure under a bushel or bury it—we're to put it to use. When the faithful servants described in the parable of the talents showed that they were trustworthy—that they were able to multiply their treasure—the master praised them, and said, "'Well done, good and faithful servant; you were faithful over a few things, I will make you ruler over many things. Enter into the joy of your lord" (Matt. 25:21).

We have been created to exalt the King of kings and to advance His kingdom upon this earth; if we do not do that, then woe unto us. How far are we going with God today? If we want to glorify Him, then we must roll up our sleeves and start advancing in the kingdom.

If there is any department in your life that is not going right, close it down. There's no time left for playing games with God—no time to sit around and become stagnant. Now is the time for every committed believer to exalt the name of our Lord Jesus Christ, to the glory of our Father in heaven, so that we can get our lives back on track and advance in His kingdom.

God has called every one of us to something special. He wants to reach out to people. We would all be on our way to hell if God hadn't reached out to us with the free gift of salvation. But He was good for it. He delivered. Why? Because, as Jesus said, God loved the world so much that He was willing to sacrifice the Lamb of God for the sins of the world. What we are is plain for God to see, and I hope it is plain to our consciences as well.

Paul says that if anyone is in Christ he is a new creation. The old nature gives way to a new and permanent nature from God, who has reconciled us to Himself through Christ. God has given us a ministry of reconciliation; God reconciles the world to Himself through the gift that Jesus Christ purchased for us on the cross of Calvary.

We are to be Christ's ambassadors to the world. God wishes to make His appeal to the people of this world through us, our testimony, and our lives. If you read Paul's challenge to the believers at Corinth (2 Cor. 5), you will have a better grasp of how God views His children. How could a righteous God whom we have offended and sinned against look at us and say, "I forgive them"? Yet, He says, "I will have mercy upon them, and I will keep them from destruction because I love them." It makes no earthly sense, but God loves us with an everlasting love.

I'm convinced that Christ will not come to a church as divided as the church in our day. If Jesus came today, there would be riots in the streets. The Baptists would rise up against the Pentecostals, the Methodists would rise up against the Baptists, the Presbyterians against the Catholics, the Catholics against the Lutherans, and the moderates against everybody. The white church would rise up against the black church and the black church against the Hispanics. The idea of any of these groups spending eternity together seems to be out of the question!

If Christ came today, there would be chaos, because we have not lived as He taught us to live. We have become backbiting, sharp-shooting, angry, and unforgiving people. We don't hate sin; we hate each other. We don't attack the forces of darkness; we attack the children of God. If Jesus were to come today, everybody would be shouting that none of the others have any right to go with Him. We wouldn't wait for God to judge the quick and the dead; we'd be doing it ourselves. There would be absolute chaos.

The Bible says that when the Lord comes, the dead in Christ shall rise up first. Then those who are alive and remain will be caught up to meet Him in the air. I tell you, if we meet in the air it will be aerial combat! Every brand of Christianity will be launching air-to-air missiles at every other brand, because we don't want anybody else to fly with us!

We have been called to reconcile with one another. That means we must sometimes go against our human nature and forgive others who may disagree with us on doctrinal issues. Our feelings don't matter—God's kingdom is not about what we feel. We are called to be peacemakers, reconcilers, and faithful stewards of the resources we've been given. God will judge each one for his offenses, and He will determine who has obeyed His commands. In the meantime, we are commanded to agree in love with all who name the name of Christ. We are to make peace despite our differences. That's what it means to be ambassadors for Christ.

Can we actually do that? Reconciliation means that we should be willing to get together and talk about what we have in common without battling over those things that would push us apart. If we put minor differences behind us, then our hearts will beat as one; we can embrace and reconcile in Christ. When we reconcile, we will have an even stronger relationship than we had before we got into a fight. Reconciliation builds alliances that make us stronger. We see each other in a different light, and we appreciate each other's strengths and weaknesses.

When we think about it, it is amazing that God would trust us to shepherd His church. The makeup of the church is incredible. There are men and women all over the world who serve God, each in his or her own way. God picked us even though He knew our temperaments, behaviors, and attitudes, and He put us all together. But He expects us to be able to put aside the things that divide us and to see each other with eyes of love so that we can build strong relationships. In that way the church will endure. The church hasn't learned these things yet, but there's no reason why we can't try a little harder.

When we learn the lesson of reconciliation, we not only gain personally, but we become a blessing to each other. Remember that Jesus has given us the ministry of reconciliation, especially for those with whom we have the greatest differences of all—those who need to be saved. We are not to stand back and scorn them; we must go among them and give a reason for the hope that is within us. We are to show them the light of Christ, share His truth, and invite them to the marriage supper of the Lamb.

That does not mean we have to approve of sin or bad behavior. Light and darkness have nothing in common. However, the people with whom we are to reconcile are in darkness. We are to share the light of Christ with them. It is also true that there are some important differences between the various denominations, and we don't have to approve of practices we believe to be in error. There are points of faith upon which we may never be able to agree. I'm not saying we should be willing to compromise our views on these things; however, we are not to fight with one another. God desires for us to be reconciled.

Remember that there was enmity between God and us at one time, but He put aside the differences and reached out to call us to the cross of Christ. We can't dance around these important issues. We need to talk about them. But we cannot forget that the King has given each of us a message of reconciliation. We are, therefore, His ambassadors, as though God were making His appeal through us alone.

FULFILLING YOUR COMMISSION

THE UNITED STATES has embassies all over the world. If an American citizen spends time in a foreign country, he or she is expected to register at the American Embassy to let it know of their presence in that country. If anything unfortunate should happen, the embassy will be able to provide assistance. The United States Government actually owns parcels of property all over the world, and other countries own parcels of land here in the United States. Wherever a nation builds an embassy, the piece of property on which the embassy is built belongs to the government of that nation.

Every ambassador to another nation is expected to make a courtesy call on the chief executive of that nation. Foreign ambassadors in this country are expected to visit the White House. They bring greetings to the president from the governing authority of the countries they represent. They receive official briefings. They have certain privileges. Our government makes it possible for the ambassadors to carry out their missions and do what they're expected to do as representatives of a foreign country.

If you and I are ambassadors for Christ, the Lord has sent us into the world as representatives of His kingdom. Every believer is a representative of God on earth. We have been called, appointed, and sent forth to represent the kingdom. We are to present a gospel that is winsome and appealing, a gospel of hope and promise, a gospel with the promise of peace with God today, and a gospel of the gift of life everlasting.

What do we actually preach, however? We preach a gospel that is harsh, critical, and judgmental. To look at the average believer one would think we serve the most depressing kingdom there can be. We want to get saved and go to heaven, but we see no value on this earth. Some of us used to be happy in the world; then we got saved—and now we go around with a long face. No wonder sinners look at us and say, "Who wants to be part of that? If that's what Christianity is all about, you can keep it!"

We say that God called us. We are ambassadors of Christ. But we act more like mourners at a funeral. Every ambassador has one main assignment: He is to be a good communicator. He needs to speak the local language. He needs to know something about the customs of the people, and he is to behave in a way that does not offend local customs. But the church has become very offensive to the lost. We put stumbling blocks in people's way. If we want to fulfill our commission, then we need to go and be reconciled to those around us so that we can call them back to God. Let them know that Jesus Christ died for their sins.

An ambassador is also supposed to be a good negotiator. He or she has to be careful about what he says, just as we who are believers need to be very careful about what we say to the unsaved. We don't want to misrepresent the kingdom of God. We have been sent to represent our sovereign Lord; when others look at us, we want them to see the beauty of the Lord. Their first impression of the kingdom of God will be what they read in our faces. The way we walk, talk, and treat each other will tell them a lot about what we're selling. Do we honestly expect them to want what we have because of what they see in us?

Jesus Christ has put His word in our mouths, and we are to bless, honor, and build up other people—not destroy them. Ambassadors know how to negotiate, and they have the authority to make binding commitments upon their government. They don't represent themselves; they represent their country. Paul says, "We are ambassadors for Christ, as though God were pleading through us" (2 Cor. 5:20).

We are to implore those who are lost in sin to be reconciled to God. We are messengers of the kingdom. Our great King is the Prince of Peace. When we are dry and thirsty, He is the water of life. He is the bread of life when we are hungry. He is the hope of the hopeless and encouragement for the downtrodden. He says, "I will never leave you nor forsake you." Not only does the King we serve set a magnificent table, but He invites us to come in and dine with Him. He never sends us into adversity alone; He follows us there. He is our shepherd. He is our rock and fortress. He is our ever-present friend in times of need. Our task, our joy, our great delight is to share the invitation of our great King with the world.

We are to tell them that a kingdom has been prepared for them. They don't have to live in darkness and sin. They can live in the light. Jesus said the kingdom of God is at hand. He meant that it has already come in Him. Those who follow the Lord don't have to submit to the rules of the kingdom of darkness. Jesus has delivered us from the kingdom of darkness. The King of kings is the head of our government.

Those who come to the King don't need a visa—the only thing they need is the mark of the washing of the blood upon their hearts. As long as they believe on the King and invite Him into their hearts, they can enjoy His bounty forever. As ambassadors, we are to tell the lost that there is room for them in the kingdom. The King didn't tell us to go and sell everything we have. He said to go and tell the people of this world that Jesus is Lord; His kingdom will endure forever.

Jesus says, "You did not choose Me, but I chose you and appointed you that you should go and bear fruit, and that your fruit should remain, that whatever you ask the Father in My name He may give you" (John 15:16). Why can't we heed His words and tell those who are outside without a Savior that the kingdom is here, today, and it is for all of them?

Let us each commit ourselves to do those things that will make the King proud of us. We serve a great King who knows how to take care of us. He has appointed us as ambassadors to the lost, and He has given us the honor and privilege of doing the work of the kingdom. He wants to live His life through us. Are you willing to do that? Will you let His responsibilities become yours? If so, you are a kingdom ambassador.

Christ is looking for women and men who want to join His diplomatic corps. I challenge you to put everything else aside and tell Him you are ready to serve. Are you winning souls for the Lord? Are you a faithful steward of the King's treasure? Are you trustworthy? Do you obey the King's command? Jesus says, "He who has My commandments and keeps them, it is he who loves Me. And he who loves Me will be loved by My Father, and I will love him and manifest Myself to him" (John 14:21).

What greater motivation could we have? Christ promises to exalt those who keep His commandments. He promises the love of the Father to all who hear His Word and obey. When we serve the King with all our heart, we will be giving what He most desires. That's how we exalt the King.

Part III:
Restoring the Kingdom

8

A City on a Hill

GOD IS IN the business of restoring lives. Whenever brothers or sisters are in distress, God asks believers to rise up and come to their aid. Unfortunately, we are so accustomed to bad news that many of us don't always respond when we hear that somebody is struggling. We expect things to be bad, so we hold back. We don't often allow ourselves to freely become the agents of blessing as God desires. We behave more like the world around us that seems to thrive on bad news. No wonder there are so many broken and wounded people out there and so much fear and pain.

Jesus said that we are the light of the world, a city on a hill that cannot be hidden (Matt. 5:14). But it sometimes takes a terrible crisis before we start to spread our light and build His kingdom. We don't want to get involved. We don't want to challenge sin and doubt. We prefer to wait for the Rapture. Without some sort of major shakeup to force us out of our comfort zone, I wonder if we'll ever see the nations come to Christ.

On one of my trips to California a few years ago I preached to a group of African believers who had a heart for international ministry. I didn't realize it at the time, but several of them were respected pastors and leaders. As a result of the meetings I attended, God began opening doors for me to teach in places that had been closed before. Why was that happening? I believe it was because the church was in turmoil, and they needed a new vision of the kingdom.

I also realized that so many Christian leaders all over the country were dealing with profound spiritual questions. They had come face to face with questions about the identity of the church, and some found that God's principles on the kingdom could give them focus and help them renew their ministries. The vision of an actual kingdom that is here in our midst would help them to confront some of the crises in the community of faith and to reevaluate some of the things they had been teaching.

At one point, God laid it on my heart to minister to a well-known Christian artist who was experiencing difficulties at the time. When I preached at the church he attended, I saw many things that encouraged me concerning his faith and commitment. But there were also some problems—brought about by those who surrounded him, their wrong judgments and misgivings—that needed to be addressed through the Word and through prayer. I went as a visiting pastor. But the pastor requested that I meet with him privately, and I left, with God's help, as a friend and brother in Christ.

This brother had many new songs to sing. But he felt as though the church was no longer interested in his music. "The sad part," he said, "is that the church is throwing the baby out with the bathwater and pushing me out into the world. That's the natural place for me to go because they love my music there. But I want to make my stand for God."

I was planning an evangelistic trip to Africa at that time, so I gave him an invitation to join me. "I believe that God has a plan for you," I said, "and I know He wants to keep you on the side of truth. Instead of Hollywood or some other opportunity in the world, maybe your new direction will come from Africa."

He gladly responded in the affirmative. He said *yes*. We went to Africa that fall and had a tremendous time of harvest and blessing. The Holy Spirit touched thousands of lives, and we truly felt the hand of God on our ministry. We were preaching and praising God, and my friend was performing great songs of faith. Tens of thousands of lives in West Africa were blessed by this man's ministry; that touched him deeply. Later he told me that he felt totally restored and refreshed. He said he believed that God had designed our meeting as a way of renewing his ministry.

Why did these things happen? Was it because Kingsley Fletcher is such a gifted man of God? Was it because I did something extraordinary? No, not at all. It was because God laid this man's name and his ministry of music on my heart, and then He prepared the time and place for me to get involved. God planned the whole thing because He had a blessing in store for both of us.

BEING TRANSPARENT WITH GOD

THAT'S HOW IT'S supposed to work in the kingdom of God. God wants us to be fruitful, and He promises to bless our efforts. The day that we turn away from our addiction to bad news and start pouring our hearts out to God, seeking His will—in our churches, in the streets, in our homes, and over the airwaves—that's the day revival will come to our land. But if we spend all our time in front of the television set, we will be consumed by bad news. It's inevitable.

The major advertising firms and marketing experts use any news or information they have to sell their product. They tell us that if we just get their products or buy their goods, then we'll feel good about ourselves; we can forget about how awful things really are. Right? But we are doing the same things in churches today. Think about it. Instead of preaching goodness and mercy and teaching people how to love one another, we settle for food and programs. Demographics and marketing tactics have overtaken the church. Such tactics do not build the kingdom; rather, they build religious country clubs.

Here in the West, we are surrounded by food, immorality, and bad news. In some of our churches, it's practically taboo to talk about evangelism and soul-winning. People don't want to speak about the blood of the Lamb. God's people are not hearing the message that God is seeking a generation of men and women who are totally sold out to Him to help renew His kingdom. Many congregations don't want to hear about fasting and prayer. They don't want to think about self-denial. They want banquets, picnics, brunches, potluck suppers, or any other excuse to celebrate the moment and avoid the necessity of becoming transparent before God.

The Bible tells us that life in the kingdom of heaven is so incredible that whenever one person is saved, the angels stop what they are doing to rejoice! It is God's passionate desire that everyone should embrace the kingdom. He knows that if we ever understand what the kingdom is all about, we will be renewed and revitalized from within. If we are reborn as people and a nation, then Christ shall reign as Lord and King. The problem is that we have not yet learned how to seek His kingdom and His righteousness; we're too busy seeking our own way, our own comfort, and our own glory.

When Jesus was teaching His disciples how to pray, He taught them the words of what we now call the Lord's prayer. Actually, we should probably call it the "Model Prayer," because it was the example He used to teach us the elements of prayer to use when we approach the Father. He taught them how simple it is to come to God in prayer, but He also wanted them to know that there is a right way and a wrong way to do it. He said that when we pray, we should speak in this manner:

> Our Father which art in heaven, hallowed be Thy name. Thy kingdom come. Thy will be done in earth, as it is in heaven. Give us this day our daily bread. And forgive us our debts, as we forgive our debtors. And lead us not into temptation, but deliver us from evil: for Thine is the kingdom, and the power, and the glory, for ever. Amen.
>
> —MATTHEW 6:9–13, KJV

How very short, but how very powerful! First, praise the Father. We tell Him we desire to see His kingdom, we desire to live by His will, and we rely upon Him for your daily bread. We trust Him to protect us from the evil one and to reign forever in power and glory.

A modern analysis identifies the elements of the model prayer as adoration, confession, thanksgiving, and supplication—ACTS, like the Book of Acts. That's a good way to remember it.

What followed next, however, may have surprised some of those standing with Jesus that day; they were not, by nature, a very forgiving people. He said:

> If you forgive men their trespasses, your heavenly Father will also forgive you. But if you do not forgive men their trespasses,

neither will your Father forgive your trespasses. Moreover, when you fast, do not be like the hypocrites, with a sad countenance. For they disfigure their faces that they may appear to men to be fasting. Assuredly, I say to you, they have their reward. But you, when you fast, anoint your head and wash your face, so that you do not appear to men to be fasting, but to your Father who is in the secret place; and your Father who sees in secret will reward you openly.

—MATTHEW 6:14–18

Remember we are talking about the kingdom. Christ is teaching His followers how to live in the kingdom. Prayer is a central part of the lives of subjects of the King; we need to be constantly in an attitude of prayer. By studying the discipline of prayer we can grasp what our relationship with God and with our fellow man is supposed to be.

RESPECTING GOD'S SOVEREIGNTY

WE ARE TO appreciate the King and bow before Him. We never lift ourselves up until the King says we may do so. A person never touches an earthly king until he touches the person. Before entering the king's chambers, there will be men outside the door who will announce his mood. They will state how to behave in his presence. Either they will say that the king is in a good mood today, so requests may be placed before him, or they warn that he is angry and will not honor requests.

A subject does not go before the king thinking that the king will do whatever is in his heart. The king's subject may not express his interests or desires unless the king acknowledges him and calls him by name. If he misbehaves or makes a serious blunder in etiquette after he has been instructed by the king's attendants, the king has the authority to have him thrown out—or worse!

Jesus said that if we seek the kingdom of God we will find it. It is God's good pleasure to give us the kingdom. But when His kingdom is revealed, there must also be an establishment of His authority. The kingdom of God will never come to a people who recognize any other authority but God's.

I Have Seen the Kingdom

When we are preaching the kingdom of God to this world, we are saying, "Father, let Your authority be established upon the earth."

When we go into the prisons and preach the gospel of the kingdom, we are saying, "God, please let Your authority be established in the hearts of men and women in this prison system."

Wherever we preach the kingdom, we are asking for the authority of God to be revealed and His power to be manifested to us.

When we preach the kingdom, we proclaim the authority of the Father as architect and builder of His own eternal domain. That's why Jesus says, "And I, if I am lifted up from the earth, will draw all peoples to Myself" (John 12:32).

When we lift Him up, we give Him the opportunity to establish His kingdom within us. When that happens, He will draw all men into the kingdom and lift up those whose hearts and lives are devoted to Him. God never forgets us. Peter reminds us that He is not slack, nor does He forget those who diligently seek after His purposes. If we lift Him up and if He draws people to Himself, then guess who comes first? We do! We humble ourselves, as James says, so He can lift us up. Humility is not a sign of stupidity or weakness; it is power under control. "And whoever exalts himself will be humbled, and he who humbles himself will be exalted" (Matt. 23:12).

If we honor Him, He will honor us. Jesus said, "This is the will of Him who sent Me, that everyone who sees the Son and believes in Him may have everlasting life; and I will raise him up at the last day" (John 6:40). "If you boldly proclaim Me," He says, "not only will I proclaim you, but I will bring you before God and proclaim you before my Father's throne."

When we come to the point of appreciating the kingdom of God, our hearts will be transformed and we will surrender to the lordship of Christ. Then, if Christ rules, He is king of all. We say also that if He is not King of all, then He is not king at all. That's why we must make Him King of our lives.

A Passport to Empowerment

WHEN WE COME to the kingdom of God in faithful obedience to

Jesus Christ, we will experience kingdom authority in our lives. If you ever try to deal with demonic forces, you will have access through praise and prayer to the armaments of heaven. But you must really be grounded in the kingdom of God and in His Word to fight in that arena. It's dangerous business and not for the faint of heart. Satan will certainly not respect us. He will eat our lunch if we let him, because he knows we don't have any authority on our own. Kingdom authority comes only to those who serve the Father and who, through fasting, prayer, and purity of heart, can wrestle with powers and principalities and overcome the devil.

If we're not kingdom warriors in good standing with the King, the Father will not allow us to tamper with His power. His power belongs to the kingdom. The use of that power is a privilege granted only to those citizens who dwell in the kingdom. That power is like a passport. It is like a mark of approval. In fact, it is a birth certificate—proof of our new birth in Christ. If we are not submitted to the lordship of Jesus Christ, it is impossible to walk with the empowerment of His kingdom.

Imagine the churches throughout the land who are not completely subject to the lordship of Jesus Christ. They want to invoke the power of Christ to overcome the darkness of this world, but they are ineffective. They wonder why they don't see better results. The answer is perfectly clear: God uses His kingdom only to establish the presence of His throne. God has in mind that His kingdom is to be revealed to those who have bowed to Him, to those who have given Him authority and dominion. If you're not experiencing kingdom power in your life, maybe you need to take a look at your passport. You may not have a visa to travel. You may not even be a subject of the King.

No one preached like Jesus preached. He preached with power and conviction; even the crowds were astonished at Him because "He taught them as one having authority, and not as the scribes" (Matt. 7:29). Jesus knew the kingdom. He was the One the Father had appointed to come and build His kingdom. He had the blueprints, so there was no doubt in His mind about what He was doing.

Over the years there have been many prophets and teachers who were called of God, and they spoke with conviction concerning the kingdom of God. Yet, they didn't have the keys of the kingdom, and they hadn't seen the blueprints. They had part of the truth, but not all of it. Only the Father has all of the truth.

What does God do from Genesis to Revelation? God uses those men and women who are totally submitted to Him, who are founded in the faith, and who are available to Him. He appoints them as prophets, priests, and kings, and He makes them kingdom builders. He calls them into service, drafts them, conscripts them out of the world, and makes them part of His program.

God says, "I want you to go and represent Me to this people. I want you to go and tell them that My kingdom has come." In the beginning, not all of them understood what that meant. Even though the prophets were the ones who were speaking the mind of the Lord, they did not have the full revelation; God had reserved that great mystery for the Son of His love. The writer of the Book of Hebrews says:

> God, who at sundry times and in divers manners spake in time past unto the fathers by the prophets, hath in these last days spoken unto us by his Son, whom he hath appointed heir of all things, by whom also he made the worlds.
>
> HEBREWS 1:1–2, KJV

You see, God gave the ministry of kingdom building to Jesus, "who being the brightness of his glory, and the express image of his person, and upholding all things by the word of his power, when he had by himself purged our sins, sat down on the right hand of the Majesty on high" (v. 3, KJV).

Jesus came to represent the kingdom. As He preached, He issued passports for all those who would believe and follow Him; in dying, He purchased our salvation.

Having purged our sins, He then returned to the Father and sat down at the right hand of God. Who is to carry out the work of building the kingdom now that Christ has risen? We are!

God gave the prophets commandments by which men were to govern the earthly kingdom. Prophets and priests proclaimed the kingdom and the Law, and anyone who violated the Law was judged guilty. Some died for not understanding the laws. But those who obeyed were given divine protection and guidance. The prophets proclaimed the Law. They spoke of the kingdom. But not one of them lived to see the full revelation of the kingdom—not until the time of John the Baptist.

When John came, he knew that God had given him a specific mission to proclaim the kingdom of God. He taught men to "repent and be baptized," even before Christ came down from Nazareth to Judea. Until that time, the Law was the guide. But when John came, he taught them a new revelation. He told them, "Repent, for the kingdom of heaven is at hand!" (Matt. 3:2). What did he mean, "at hand"? He meant that the kingdom was very near—as close as your own hand.

No other prophet had such a compelling revelation for the kingdom of God. But there was a price to pay. When John the Baptist's work was completed, he had to get out of the way so that there would be no distractions—so that the kingdom of God, in Christ, could be revealed. John had prepared the way for the One to come. That was his ministry—to make straight the way of the Lord.

John was the prophet who was privileged to bring the Law and the kingdom together. When Jesus learned that King Herod had thrown John into prison, He gave him a remarkable tribute, saying, "For I say to you, among those born of women there is not a greater prophet than John the Baptist" (Luke 7:28).

When John had finished his work, he became an offering to the Lord. He was beheaded at the request of Herod's stepdaughter, Salome, and her wicked mother. The prophet who had announced the kingdom of Christ was humiliated and cruelly murdered.

Today, we say we want to serve God. We say, "Oh, God, I'll do anything for you!" But are we as committed to serving the kingdom as John the Baptist? Are we really ready to make the kind of sacrifice he was called on to make? Think about it.

The Ministry of Love

MAYBE THE KINGDOM is not what you think it is. It is not designed to bring glory to us. It's not some ethereal fairy land where all our dreams come true. This may come as a shock to some people, but God is not lying awake all night worrying about what He can do to make us happy!

Oh, yes, He loves us, and He has a plan for us that can bring us great peace and joy if we're faithful and obedient. But it may not include wealth and privilege and all the comforts of this world. It probably will not include fame and fortune. Chances are it won't include many of the earthly pleasures we dream about. In fact, it could even cost our lives. Still interested?

Jesus said the kingdom is more than meat and drink. It has three characteristics—righteousness, peace, and joy; all of these are wrapped in the Holy Ghost. But some of us don't want to go where God tells us to go. We don't want to do what He has in mind. That's why it's so difficult for so many people to accept the call of God on their lives. They fear that if He calls them, He will send them off to be missionaries in Africa. They're afraid to obey God, but they want to live in the kingdom. But I must ask you: How can you be a kingdom citizen if you don't play by the rules?

The church is full of people who want all the frills and comforts of faith but none of the burdens. They have not come to the place of total submission to the King. But look at John the Baptist. He closed the chapter of the Law and brought to an end the Old Covenant of blood sacrifice. How? By giving his own blood. He became an innocent sacrifice of the Law.

When Jesus heard that John was dead, He grew quiet. He left and went back to Galilee to be alone for a time. He knew that John had closed a chapter in the history of the kingdom. Now it was time for Christ to come forth and introduce the New Covenant and the rule of the kingdom in our daily lives. What a tremendous opportunity, but what a great cost it would soon entail. Jesus too would have to die a horrible death to fulfill His mission.

Of all those born of woman, Jesus said, there was never a prophet greater than John the Baptist. But in His very next words, Jesus said, "But he who is least in the kingdom of God is greater than [he]" (Luke 7:28). Why would He say that? He praises John as the greatest of all the prophets, and then He says that any ordinary believer, no matter how weak or insecure, is greater than John the

Baptist! Can that be so? You see, John came to end the authority of the Law as the medium of reconciliation with God. His role was to introduce an entirely new order: a New Covenant.

Paul explains it this way: "For by grace you have been saved through faith, and that not of yourselves; it is the gift of God, not of works, lest anyone should boast" (Eph. 2:8–9). Under the old order, the only hope of salvation came by keeping the Law. It was, in a sense, a salvation based on works. If you broke even one law, you were judged guilty of breaking all the law. No one could be saved by the Law alone. There was no dispensation of grace.

By the light of Christ, we see that the purpose of the Law was to reveal our sin and draw us to repentance. But not until the sacrifice of Christ upon the cross was there an offering substantial enough to appease the wrath and the righteous anger of a holy God. John prophesied Messiah's coming; Christ completed the sacrifice.

John the Baptist gave his blood to seal the Law. Jesus said, "Do not think that I came to destroy the Law or the Prophets. I did not come to destroy but to fulfill" (Matt. 5:17). Jesus interpreted and completed the Law. He was the fulfillment. That means that within the Law there was a deed of transmission. The Law contained a will that had been locked up for ages, and no one seemed to know it was there. John the Baptist said, "He who is coming after me is mightier than I, whose sandals I am not worthy to carry. He will baptize you with the Holy Spirit and fire" (Matt. 3:11). Jesus said, "I have come that they may have life, and that they may have it more abundantly" (John 10:10).

When Jesus went down to the Jordan River to be baptized by John, John recognized Him as the anointed Son of God, and he tried to deter Him, saying, "I need to be baptized by You, and are You coming to me?" But Jesus said, "Permit it to be so now, for thus it is fitting for us to fulfill all righteousness" (Matt. 3:14–15). Then John went ahead and performed the sacred rite of baptism for the Savior of mankind.

John was interested in knowing the will of the Father, but it was not meant for John to receive the full revelation of the kingdom of God. Jesus prayed, "I thank You, Father, Lord of heaven and earth, that You have hidden these things from the wise and prudent and have revealed them to babes" (Matt. 11:25). He said, "Many prophets and righteous men desired to see what you see, and did not see it, and to hear what you hear, and did not hear it" (Matt. 13:17).

Those who came later have understanding denied to the prophets and righteous men who came earlier. Are we therefore to believe that we now understand the kingdom and have full knowledge of what it's all about? No, not yet. Not many of us are really prepared to make the personal sacrifice that generally comes with absolute submission to the King. If we really make a commitment to live in the kingdom, work in the kingdom, and keep the covenants of the kingdom, we may have to endure times of stress. We may have to go without. We may even have to face death.

John proclaimed that the kingdom was at hand. He later died. Jesus came as our Savior and revealed the kingdom. He died. Paul came to reveal the mysteries of the kingdom that had been hidden for ages. He died, too. All the disciples and apostles of Jesus, with the sole exception of John who was appointed to write the Book of Revelation, died an agonizing death. They were martyred for their faith—every one of them.

We can't talk about the kingdom and claim to be part of what God is doing unless we understand the risks. We may live a life of peace and tranquility—or we may be facing death. Those who come by the blood of the Lamb and the word of their testimony— who love not their lives unto death—are those who know what the kingdom of God is like. These are the ones who understand the will of the kingdom.

However, if we understand the will of the kingdom, we will not be afraid of those who threaten our physical lives. We will not fear those who mock or laugh when we proclaim the Word of God. We will not be embarrassed when our family kicks us out and tells us that we're crazy for believing in Jesus. If we understand the kingdom, nothing man can do will destroy us. We will not be afraid of the ones that can kill the flesh.

PEACE, JOY, RIGHTEOUSNESS

THIS IS NOT the image most people have of the kingdom. It's not the kind of commitment many of us are willing to make. That's why Jesus says, "Many are called, but few chosen" (Matt. 20:16). We cannot understand this kind of thinking unless our minds are renewed. Paul said that we are to be transformed by the renewing of our minds, so that we may prove what is good and acceptable, and the perfect will of God (Rom. 12:1–2). But unless we live in the kingdom, that can't happen.

The kingdom of God is not meat and drink but righteousness. *Righteousness* is not holiness; it means having a right standing with God. We have to be righteous before we can pursue holiness. Through the former, we have been privileged to stand before God. If I were to ask you if you are filled with the Holy Spirit, I would be asking if you are walking in His righteousness. If you are a child of God and live in His kingdom, then you are judged to be righteous. If you have been "born again," then you have been judged righteous. Not because of anything you have done, but because of what Christ has done for you.

God cannot look upon man's unrighteousness, so He sent Christ as our Mediator. In the eyes of a holy God, all our righteousness is as filthy rags. When we come to the kingdom, Christ changes our direction. He gives us a new name and a new identity. He says, "I am giving you My passport. You have credit with the Father using My credit card." God says, "I accept you in My kingdom by virtue of your relationship with My Son. You are righteous and complete in Him."

That's how we begin our journey of faith. That's how our guilt is removed. That's how we make peace with God. The peace that God gives is the will of His kingdom. The world talks about peace all the time. It riots for peace! But it doesn't have the kind of peace God gives. The world doesn't even know what true peace means. You see, peace doesn't mean happiness. Money may not buy love, but it can buy happiness. We can drink and be happy for a while. We can eat and be happy until we're hungry again. We can go on vacation and be happy. But that's not peace. The peace and joy that come to the child of the King is something that money can't buy, and it's everlasting. If we live in the kingdom of God, we live in the peace, joy, and imputed righteousness of Christ; nothing man can do can ever take those things away from us.

We have God's greatest gifts because of our right standing with Him through Christ. Something inside us says, "Don't panic. The King is on His throne!"

Jesus will lead us. He will direct us and say, "Don't be afraid, My child. For I will never leave you nor forsake you." For those who don't live in the kingdom, the opposite is true. They will panic. They should panic! They will be nervous wrecks. Without the peace that only faith in Jesus Christ can bring, everything will frighten them. Personal criticism will destroy them. Failures will devastate them. Matters of life and death will haunt and terrify them. They do not have the peace that passes all understanding.

If we know our standing in the kingdom of God, then the peace of Christ takes over our lives and gives us the ability to rest completely in Him. Jesus says, "Peace I leave with you, My peace I give to you; not as the world gives do I give to you. Let not your heart be troubled, neither let it be afraid" (John 14:27). This world cannot grasp real peace. The peace of Christ is everlasting and undeniable. It is the peace that comes from knowing that sin and death no longer have any power. We have been set free. Jesus says, "If the Son makes you free, you shall be free indeed" (John 8:36).

Are you peaceful today? You should be, if you're a citizen of the kingdom. If you understand the peace of God, you will be filled with joy. That doesn't mean you'll go around laughing and giggling all the time. If you laugh too much, that could mean you've got a problem! We live in a society that is addicted to laughter and silliness. That's not what Christ offers. He offers a deep-down joy that comes from knowing we are citizens of the kingdom, our futures are secure, and we will have peace with God forever and ever. If we know the One who is on the throne, we know that our sins are forgiven; anytime we come into the presence of the King, we will experience the fullness of His peace, joy, and righteousness.

The joy of the Lord is our strength. David declares, "You will show me the path of life; in Your presence is fullness of joy; at Your right hand are pleasures forevermore" (Ps. 16:11). Jesus knew what He had to do; that's why He resisted those who wanted to make him King before His time.

When He died and rose again, He showed Himself to be Lord of lords and King of kings. "Now," He said, "you can identify Me as the King. My kingdom is now established," He said, and before ascending into heaven, He told them, "All authority has been given to Me in heaven and on earth. Go therefore and make disciples of all the nations, baptizing them in the name of the Father and of the Son and of the Holy Spirit, teaching them to observe all things that I have commanded you; and lo, I am with you always, even to the end of the age" (Matt. 28:18–20). He said it was the Father's will to grant them the kingdom.

How stubborn we are. We say Jesus is Lord, yet we don't obey His commands. The King says, "Go into the highways, and as many as you find, invite to the wedding." He has commissioned us to go to the nations and tell whoever will hear the Word of God that the kingdom is at hand. We are to say that the peace, joy, and righteousness of our King is available to all who will come. He is looking for people who will worship Him. But often we don't go. We fail Him. We hide His words in our hearts and put our light under a bushel.

Jesus cries out to us, "You say you are the children of My kingdom, yet you do not do as I have commanded. You are supposed to let your light so shine before men that they will see your good works and glorify your Father who is in heaven! Why aren't you doing that?"

If we are children of the kingdom, then why don't we go into the cities as salt and light and build the kingdom? Without salt, the world has nothing to preserve it. Without light, the lost cannot see the way.

Jesus says, "My people are living in sin and guilt; they need to know that there is a Savior who has paid the price for their sin. There is hope. There is deliverance. There is peace. Go and tell them they can have My peace." But we keep the peace that God has given us to ourselves. We think the kingdom is ours alone, and we don't share it with others. How can we call Him Lord when we do not do what He commands?

Speak to Him now, will you? "Father, you know that I love You. I have heard Your Word, and I have claimed Your promise of eternal life. Forgive me, Lord, for failing to take Your truth to heart. Forgive me for failing to be salt and light to a world that is dying in darkness. Forgive me for putting myself and my own interests ahead of You and Your interests. Lord Jesus, put me back on the right track." Will you do that? Will you make that your prayer today?

BEFORE THE DARKNESS FALLS

GOD DOES NOT want us sitting around waiting for the end to come. He's not going to send His chariots to rapture you out of this world so we can run off and get all the treasures we've been laying up in heaven. That's not the plan. He didn't build the kingdom just to give us a promotion. He's looking down on us at this very moment, and He's watching to see what we've been doing with His Word. He says, "Get up, get out there, and make disciples."

What is this kingdom all about anyway? The King has called us to spread the Word and share His grace with the lost. But perhaps you're just sitting there doing nothing—whispering, "Send somebody, Lord. Send somebody else, Lord."

The King says, "I have more room in My kingdom, and I want you to invite others to join Us. I love them, too, just as I love you." Maybe you're timid and a little shy about talking about your majestic King. You're afraid somebody might think you're strange or say that you're just trying to push your morality down their throats.

Let me say something to you: We dare not go into the presence of a king and fall asleep. Try it once, and it will be the longest nap ever taken—we won't wake up. We go before a king attentive, with open ears, open heart, open mind, and open eyes. If we come into the presence of a king, we won't be bored, and we won't be in any hurry to leave, either. We'll sit there until he's ready for us to leave. If the king tells us to go and do something, we'll get up and do it as quickly and as well as we know how. We wouldn't dare refuse. So, if we would do that for an earthly king, why aren't we doing it for the greatest King of all?

God has so much to teach us. He wants us to help extend His kingdom. It is up to us to spread the Word and call those who are lost to the mercy seat of Christ. Christ has asked us—commissioned us—to go forth. Are we doing it? When we pray, "Thy kingdom come; Thy will be done," what are we really saying? If we're not saying that we are available to do the Father's will, then we're just speaking empty platitudes.

Jesus said that the night is coming when no man will be able to do the work of the kingdom. That should be a sober warning. Time is running out, and God is watching today to see what's on our minds. Since we have so little light left in this world, shouldn't we be spreading the light of Christ? Let us lift up a torch that will never fail. Let us raise up a city on a hill and spread the light of God's truth before the darkness falls.

We have eyes to see and ears to hear. Will we take our passport of faith and go out into all the world to make disciples for our King? I ask you to stop now and pray these words; think about what you're saying: "Thy kingdom come. Thy will be done in earth, as it is in heaven." Amen.

9

Of Such Is the Kingdom

WHEN I CAME to America, I left so many things behind. I left dreams, comforts, and many future privileges. I deprived myself of the joy that was set before me and came here, not for the American dream, but with a dream for America. My vision for America today is that she will go back, short term, so she can go forward. Whenever you're traveling on the highway and miss the turn and lose your way, the best thing to do is to go back to where you went wrong and get back on the right way.

I see myself as a sent-back "Thank You" to the generation of the founding fathers of America; I am the fruit of their labors. There are many more that God will send back to speak to America's spiritual conscience. The seed that was planted in my native land by Christian missionaries from the West many years ago has now grown up into a generation of Christian men and women who love God and who recognize Jesus Christ as the only Way, the only Truth, and the only Life. I have come to America to say thank you, but it is a challenging mission that I consider a privilege and which gives me great pleasure.

It is obvious that there is a stress in the nations today—including my new country. We no longer have the clear vision given to us by the grandfathers and founding fathers of the land. I am here as a reminder of the time when you were on the right path. What you shared with my fathers has now flourished. The fruit you planted in

I Have Seen the Kingdom

Africa is now in harvest. The truth you shared with my native people has spread to millions of lives throughout the entire continent of Africa; today my fathers and my brothers and sisters in Africa rejoice in that truth.

A wise man will not reject the inheritance left to him by his fathers. Why would America reject the treasure her fathers prepared? Just a few years ago the American people understood the majesty of that heritage. Your former president, John F. Kennedy, said in his inaugural address, "The rights of man come not from the generosity of the state but from the hand of God." But today I see that many people in this country seem to believe that the state is their god, that government is their salvation.

On the walls of the Jefferson Memorial in this nation's capital I have read these words: "God who gave us life gave us liberty." Those are not the words of preachers—not of Jonathan Edwards or Dwight L. Moody—but of Thomas Jefferson, your patriot and a founding father, author of the Declaration of Independence, and third president of the United States. The inscription goes on to say, "Can the liberties of a nation be secure when we have removed a conviction that these liberties are the gift of God?"

I come here as a son of Africa—born, bred, and reared in my father's household by godly parents with a vision of truth, with a faith in God they learned from you—but has America lost that vision? Have you forgotten that truth? Have you thrown away that clear understanding of your obligations to the kingdom of Jesus Christ?

If so, I can see why you have fallen so far. I can understand why crime is raging in the streets of your cities. I can see why divorce, child abuse, domestic violence, and out-of-wedlock childbirths are out of control in America. I can begin to understand how some of you have failed to understand the deep and awful consequences of taking innocent human lives.

If you have forgotten your heritage, America, then I weep for you. But I have come to remind you of the truth your forefathers understood. I have come to commend to you the Lord of lords and King of kings, the Redeemer who can still redeem this great nation and restore you to your former honor and glory.

I have a dream for America that one day her great-grandchildren will affirm with one resounding voice, "What my fathers stood for is still true!" I dream that from the red hills of Georgia to the rocky bluffs of Puget Sound the great-grandsons and great-granddaughters of former slaves will recommit themselves to the hopes and dreams of those who suffered for their freedom. I dream that they too will stand firm, renew their passion for the Way, the Truth, and the Life—for the Savior who gave His life to set men free.

I am here to encourage America, to stir you up, to provoke you to come back to the faith of your fathers. I say to you, "Yes, God will bless America if America will come back to the faith of her fathers. But if America no longer will believe in the God of her fathers, then Americans have no right to inherit His blessing." You cannot claim your inheritance when you are working every day to destroy everything for which your fathers stood! If I may give a gentle challenge—don't let any stranger take away your inheritance!

Come back to your inheritance, because that legacy will tell from what kind of stock you are. How you use what your forefathers left you will tell the whole world of what you are made. You must know that if you intend to claim the blessings of your forefathers, you cannot ignore their faith; it was their resilient Christian faith that brought them the abundance you now enjoy—they bought you the privileges you now take for granted.

I am an example of the faith in which your forefathers believed. Some of them came to my country and shared their faith with my great-grandfathers. Some of them—many of them—lived and died there in Africa. Just as Jesus shed His blood for me, they gave their blood for me so that I might know the truth and claim my birthright of freedom.

They did not do this in vain; they did it for the redemption of my people. If their teachings could deliver my forefathers from idolatry and help give me the blessing of peace with God, then I say to you, *their seed,* to receive your patrimony. Idolatry was no good for Africa, and it is no good for you either. My hope is that America will come back to the kingdom of God while there is still time.

Please hear this important word: The kingdom of God is not coming. It is not far off. *It is here now.* What did Jesus say? Mark says, "Jesus came to Galilee, preaching the gospel of the kingdom of God, and saying, 'The time is fulfilled, and the kingdom of God is at hand. Repent, and believe in the gospel'" (Mark 1:14–15). The kingdom of God is within you (Luke 17:21).

Matthew tells us, "Jesus went about all the cities and villages, teaching in their synagogues, preaching the gospel of the kingdom, and healing every sickness and every disease among the people" (Matt. 9:35). Jesus said that the kingdom of God is not of this world, but it is very real. It is the kingdom of God's truth and righteousness, and it is here now, at this very minute! It is in our midst, and we are stewards of that heavenly kingdom.

America, I beg you, come back to the kingdom. God is as concerned for the one sheep that is lost as He is for the ninety-nine who are safe in the fold. Once you were in the fold; you were safe once. You sent your sons and daughters to preach the gospel to the world. But today, *you* are the lost sheep. *You* are the ones that have strayed from the fold. God desires to call you back to His pasture and to the safety of His truth. Will you hear Him? Will you return? Will you rest once again in the love of the Good Shepherd?

SLAVERY: THE PUNISHMENT OF GOD

WHEN ANY GROUP of people know and serve God, they are blessed by Him. But the moment they turn against Him, they become victims of slavery. It may be slavery to passions and lusts or slavery to other nations, but the result of our unfaithfulness to the Creator is always a form of bondage. It happened to the Jews; it happened to the Indians. It even happened to the Africans. It's impossible for those who know the Lord to turn away without entering into bondage. "And even as they did not like to retain God in their knowledge, God gave them over to a debased mind" (Rom. 1:28).

I want to say something here for your consideration. Even though it may sound controversial for some people, let's read it with an open mind. Slavery was something by which God chastised the people of Israel when they went against Him. (See Hebrews 12:5–8.) The Scriptures make it clear that God used plagues, military invasion, conquest, and even captivity and slavery in a foreign land as punishment for rebellion against Him and for the sin of idolatry.

Whenever a people worship idols—either by ignorance or on purpose—the fact remains that they have turned away from the one true God to honor their man-made gods. (See Exodus 20:3.) They lose patience with a God who they think works slowly over time; they want their gratification instantly. This is often the first step on the road to slavery.

By the time slavery came to Africa, our fathers were like the Indians—the Aztecs and Mayas. They were like the Egyptians and the people of Israel. They had a love for God; they were worshipers. But our fathers turned to idolatry, which enslaved them. The spirit of slavery always begins with idolatry.

In other words, for four hundred years in Egypt and seventy years in Babylon, the children of Israel were in bondage as slaves because of the sins of their fathers. We know that. It is clearly stated in the Bible. It is also a fact of history. But when our world today talks about slavery, they don't think about it in spiritual terms but purely on the grounds of judgment, greed, and the abuse of the human will and spirit. They don't think about slavery as a kind of judgment or as the result of the sins of their fathers in Africa. As a black African, a pastor, and a lover of history, I can share with you that God's original intent was not for man to dominate another human being. He intended to rule over our hearts with love, righteousness, peace, and joy in the Holy Spirit. He wanted to share dominion with us. But man's sin changed man's benefits.

They abandoned the living God and started worshiping the sun, moon, stars, and idols of wood and stone. God has said that idolatry is abominable to Him. He will always judge those who indulge in idol worship. Anytime a person knows God and refuses to acknowledge Him as God, He will give him over to a reprobate mind. (See Romans 1:28.)

God allows and permits evil—but He never connives with evil. He allows things to happen for our ultimate good. We look at the past *for history*—God looks to the future *for triumph*.

Some of the early African chiefs who saw the profitability of slavery were not only acting upon their own greed and wickedness—they were also used of God to preserve a next generation. "But as for you, ye thought evil against me; but God meant it unto good, to bring to pass, as it is this day, to save much people alive" (Gen. 50:20, KJV).

The people that were taken to America and Europe as slaves were actually the Moseses and Josephs of Africa. They were taken into slavery so that they could go ahead and prepare a way of freedom for their people. In fact, if more American blacks really understood the whole picture, if they could truly see their own place in the light of God's triumphal end, they would not complain about being here. They would rejoice! They would praise God that, through the terrible instrument of slavery, they were allowed to come and make a way for the people of the world!

Besides the fact and feelings that accompany these atrocities, let us now consider what I believe is the real spiritual meaning. Slavery brings deep spiritual hurts, deep spiritual pain, and many other spiritual manifestations to the enslaved person.

Because of idolatry and other abominations, God was about to send famine, pestilence, and plague upon the entire continent of Africa as His judgment against our fathers who had sinned against heaven. Since He is a just God, before He unleashed His fury upon the land, He first sent the seed of Africa away to a place of safety so they would not be contaminated by the sins of their fathers. This was also to preserve them for another generation. Yes, some died horribly on the ships and never made it to land. But God's eternal plan was intact.

Remember the illustration of the country of Australia. It was begun when England sent her castoffs—undesirable men and women and the overflow of criminals from her prisons—to exile in the wild, untamed land down under. From that wretched beginning, God preserved a seed that has risen to stand on an equal basis with the world. Remember: "But as for you, ye thought evil against me; but God meant it unto good, to bring to pass, as it is this day, to save much people alive" (Gen. 50:20, KJV).

Very few black Americans have thought of these things, however, and I'm sure there are many who have become so accustomed to focusing on slavery as a great evil that they have lost sight of the good that was accomplished.

I believe this view of slavery that God has given to me through prayer and His Word will not only restore to God the glory He deserves for His mercy and providence, but it should also serve as a first step toward racial reconciliation in this country.

What did God say to the children of Israel in Deuteronomy 8? "Be careful to follow every command I am giving you today, so that you may live and increase and may enter and possess the land that the LORD promised on oath to your forefathers" (v. 1, NIV).

Then He says, "Remember how the LORD your God led you all the way in the desert these forty years, to humble you and to test you in order to know what was in your heart, whether or not you would keep his commands. He humbled you..." (Deut. 8:2–3, NIV). Though the people were humbled, He also brought them into a land of plenty with all kinds of pleasant things. But then God offers this strong warning:

> Then it shall be, if you by any means forget the LORD your God, and follow other gods, and serve them and worship them, I testify against you this day that you shall surely perish. As the nations which the LORD destroys before you, so you shall perish, because you would not be obedient to the voice of the LORD your God.
>
> —DEUTERONOMY 8:19–20

This was done for our example so that we would not do what our early Egyptian and other African fathers did, and so that God could preserve a remnant of His people. One of the things black America doesn't know is that they have been protected. Yes, by the vehicle of slavery, just like the children of Israel before us, we are part of a seed, a remnant, that God was preserving in order to help Africa one day to introduce the realities of freedom and success to the continent.

Tell them your story! You are their Moses, their Joseph. Why did it happen? Because God was about to shake the continent of Africa from one end to the other with righteous indignation and justice. God has the right to shake anything that can be shaken. Our forefathers were destroyed by the devastation; some of the slavery was necessary as a means of protecting the seed of future generations.

I Have Seen the Kingdom

Listen to me, my African brothers and sisters: When our grand-fathers and grandmothers were forced to come to this continent and to the islands of the New World, they wept for the ancient land, just as the Bible says of the Jews. Read Psalm 137 and just think of the parallels with your own story:

> By the rivers of Babylon we sat and wept
>   when we remembered Zion.
> There on the poplars
>   we hung our harps,
> for there our captors asked us for songs,
>   our tormentors demanded songs of joy;
>   they said, "Sing us one of the songs of Zion!"
>
> How can we sing the songs of the Lord
>   while in a foreign land?
> If I forget you, O Jerusalem,
>   may my right hand forget its skill.
> May my tongue cling to the roof of my mouth
>   if I do not remember you,
> if I do not consider Jerusalem
>   my highest joy.
>
> Remember, O Lord, what the Edomites did
>   on the day Jerusalem fell.
> "Tear it down," they cried,
>   "tear it down to its foundations!"
>
> O Daughter of Babylon, doomed to destruction,
>   happy is he who repays you
>   for what you have done to us—
> he who seizes your infants
>   and dashes them against the rocks.
>
> —NIV

The parallels with what happened to Africa are only too clear—they are a true demonstration of God's hand. Listen to me, my black brothers and sisters: This is how He works. This is how God has preserved you and your people through the generations.

The people of Israel cried out, "They require of us a song, but how can we sing the Lord's song in a strange land?" Yes, and the Negro spirituals born in America, rich with the language and the sounds of Africa, filled the air day and night on the plantations. Everybody, black and white, loved those melodies; they were alive with the spirit of African music and customs.

The people sang, even as they wept, like the slaves of Babylon, over the land they had left forever. And I say to my black brothers and sisters in this land that I believe it was those same godly people who were the means by which God spared the people of my own country. Through your forefathers He saved a remnant from destruction.

As the black men on the plantations worked throughout the day, they sang. As their women worked in the big house or picked cotton in the fields, they sang. It was their strength; it was their music that gave them the courage to go on day after day. Today most black Americans don't think of this; they don't realize how special they are to God, that they were sent in those wretched ships to a new land so that their seed could be spared.

My word to black Americans is this: Let go of your anger and outrage. Release your wounded spirit. The dignity of a black man or woman comes from God—not from man. We cannot shake our fist at God and merely look at what we have here in this land. Don't take it for granted. We must make use of the many outstanding gifts and talents that God has given to us. We are achieving great success—God is turning the evil to good. The poorest person in America has ten times more than many of the richest people in the lands from which our ancestors came.

God always judges the nation that enslaves people. Once He sets a people free, He returns wealth and ability to them to rebuild a community of people. But Joseph did not return to Israel to build his life—he built his life in Egypt. We don't need the ships to return us back to Africa—we are to build our futures here. We are to establish a community here that is not built on racial lines—but on kingdom principles. And as we rebuild here, God will enable us to send a portion of our strength and material blessings back to our homeland also.

167

I Have Seen the Kingdom

If there is a people who can understand the principles of a kingdom culture, who can teach God's kingdom principles, it is the black people. I wish black America would hear her name being called and lift up her head—her dignity is being restored and God has abundant blessings in store for her in the future. The church must come back to God while there is still time. Listen to the words of Paul in Acts 17, where he is speaking to the rulers of Athens:

> The God who made the world and everything in it is the Lord of heaven and earth and does not live in temples built by hands. And he is not served by human hands, as if he needed anything, because he himself gives all men life and breath and everything else. From one man he made every nation of men, that they should inhabit the whole earth; and he determined the times set for them and the exact places where they should live. God did this so that men would seek him and perhaps reach out for him and find him, though he is not far from each one of us.
>
> —ACTS 17:24–27, NIV

Do you hear what Paul is saying? From one man, Adam, God made every nation of men—black, white, brown, and yellow—and God determined where they would live upon the earth. For each of them He set the times for their societies to rise and fall, and He determined before the world was formed the exact places where they should live. Now, would we argue with Paul and say, "Well, surely God didn't know about slavery!"? Of course He did; He sent the children of Israel into slavery, time and time again, including their four hundred years in Egypt.

In fact, God told them precisely how long their captivity would last. "Know certainly," God said, "that your descendants will be strangers in a land that is not theirs, and will serve them, and they will afflict them four hundred years" (Gen. 15:13). God also said that after their return from the house of bondage He would judge the nation that had enslaved them. Is that what is happening here? Is America being punished for her two hundred years of slavery? It certainly seems like it.

Of Such Is the Kingdom

A Vital, Dynamic Faith

ARE BLACKS IN America still in bondage today? No. Their great-great-grandparents were freed from the yoke of slavery more than one hundred thirty years ago by Abraham Lincoln in 1865. The Civil War was fought and six hundred thousand people shed their blood to purchase their freedom. That is no small thing; people need to understand what a great price slavery has already cost this nation.

In economic, social, and political terms bondage still exists. Some are still enslaved in self-imposed slavery—children born out of wedlock, homes susceptible to violence, irresponsibility, and rebellion.

The system is inadequate, that is true, and life is still difficult for many black people in this country. There are no longer slaves in America. Freedom has been given to every person who claims America as home. But please remember these words of Scripture:

> And He has made from one blood every nation of men to dwell on all the face of the earth, and has determined their preappointed times and the boundaries of their dwellings, so that they should seek the Lord, in the hope that they might grope for Him and find Him, though He is not far from each one of us.
> —ACTS 17:26–27

What God has done is amazing. And He will not do anything without a witness. If America should choose not to serve God, then He will look to another place. In fact, many believe He is doing that already. Look at what He did in Europe. Those nations were once the stronghold of the Christian faith: Italy, Germany, France, Spain, England, Ireland, Scotland, and Wales. They were nations where Christianity was very strong, where the people loved God. They worshiped Him. But now their zeal has declined. A new generation arose that did not recognize the efforts of its fathers, and they put out the revival fires.

Today those countries are cold to the things of God. They have lost their first love. They are nations of atheists and socialists who are at this moment removing all evidence of their former faith and the Christian religion from public view. They no longer love or worship the Creator as they once did. They no longer enjoy His blessing.

Has God left Himself without a witness? Not at all. He has simply turned away from those who no longer seek Him, and He has given America great opportunities to share His witness with the world through prosperity. But if the people of this nation succeed in what they now call "the separation of church and state," if they succeed in throwing God out of all areas of public life, and if the churches do indeed "redefine" and "reimagine" the doctrines of our faith and fail to serve God with all their heart, mind, soul, and strength, then hold on, my brothers and sisters, because God will not hang around long when those who worship Him grow silent. God is not desperate—He is all-sufficient.

What we are struggling with in America today is very, very serious. I hope you know it. The attempt to evict God from our lives is a very serious game with very serious, long-range consequences. If we truly understood what is at risk, I believe people would repent and turn back to God before consequential judgment comes.

If that happened, we would see revival exploding all around us! There would be an awakening of faith like nothing this world has ever seen! Is there time? Can it happen? Oh, I hope and pray it may! That's why it is so urgent that we come back to the basics and seek first the kingdom of God and His righteousness with all our hearts.

When I preached this message recently at a gathering of believers in Florida, it caused many to return to God. The message was shown on their television broadcast continually, and people have been calling our ministry office about it ever since. One man said to me, "This message needs to go to the whole world." People have said that this message would free both the black man and the white man. The white man is intimidated by the black, and the black man is bitter about the white. But unless we can get blacks and whites to work and worship together inside the church, then we can hardly expect those outside the church to live in harmony.

The church is a reflection of society, but she is also an influence on it. We are the salt of the earth and the light of the world; we are a lamp; and we are the shining city on a hill. But too often we Christians are intimidated by the world and are not willing to let our light so shine before men that they will see our good works and glorify our Father in heaven.

A lot of believers today are hiding out in churches, making pious pronouncements like, "Take the whole world, but just give me Jesus!" They think that's good and holy. But I can tell you, that is not what Jesus has in mind. First of all, if we're willing to relinquish the world, the devil says, "Fantastic! I'll take it." And he really has a firm hold on it now.

If we give Satan the world, how can we influence the nations? Jesus said that our light must not be hidden; we are to be salt and light. We are to go to all the world, making disciples and baptizing them in the name of the Father, Son, and Holy Spirit. That is not a passive act. That is risky business, one which demands confrontation with evil. It demands that we look into the eyes of the world and call them to repentance. That's why only a vital, dynamic faith will do.

Except for a resurgence of faith in those Eastern European countries that suffered so long and so brutally under communist repression, very little is happening in Europe today. There is little evidence of the kingdom of God from the North Sea to the Adriatic; from all I can see the continent of Europe is spiritually dead. The revival taking place in Great Britain today is very small compared to where she came from. Despite the claims of a few evangelists, the prospect of an all-out awakening seems unrealistic. Yes, individual lives are being touched. And there's an opening in mainline evangelical churches as well as in other African churches. That is true. But it's not a general awakening. As much as I hate to say it, I believe God is finished with Europe in terms of spiritual leadership, though He may yet save a remnant to be the pillar for the next generation.

THAT SOME MAY BE SAVED

AMERICA HAS BEEN used of the Lord tremendously, and there are still some monies going from this place to build up the church in other lands. I believe that one of the main reasons God blessed this nation and allowed such tremendous wealth to be gained here was so that His kingdom could be spread to the ends of the earth. God saved

I Have Seen the Kingdom

America so that the kingdom of God could be established in every nation.

My prayer today is that America will be saved and that she will return to her only just and righteous King. I came here with a dream for America. Those who cherished the American dream have come already, and they have had their moment of glory. Many struggled, fought, bled, and died that the dream of prosperity and freedom might thrive on these shores.

Those who come now to your shores are coming to interpret your dreams. I, as one of them, have come with a dream *for* America. If it should happen that I would be required to shed my own blood for America, I would gladly do so in gratitude for the gift of eternal life your fathers and mothers helped to give me through their obedience to the heavenly vision. There is life in the seed, and in every fruit there is life. If I am the fruit of their labor, then I would not hesitate to sacrifice anything required of me—including my life—if I could help bring about the redemption of this nation.

It breaks my heart to see so many young American blacks, influenced by the nation of Islam, who are buying into the belief that Christianity is the white man's religion. They are reacting in anger and fear because of the pain they have been through. When a person has lived with pain for a very long time, they may learn to ignore the pain. They learn to bear it in silence.

But the moment they are reminded of the pain, they consider the one who inflicted the pain to be an enemy. At times pain is necessary to give you an opportunity to really appreciate the other side of things. Without pain there is no gain. Pain in itself is not bad; it makes you appreciate your former state, or it prepares you for some kind of change.

There are no more godly people on this planet than black Americans who truly know the Lord, and their worship expression is pure. But it is tragic to see the outrage that has developed in some of the black communities. The bitterness and divisiveness of our day—aggravated by the hatred coming from groups that want to exploit that outrage—are stealing blacks away from the faith that has nurtured and sustained them for centuries, a faith that is so natural to them.

Of Such Is the Kingdom

My greatest concern is that blacks might somehow allow their anger to dislodge them from their faith in Jesus Christ, who is the Lord of lords and King of kings. When a person has been through the fire, that person's passions are purified. The purity of worship comes out of the expression of pain.

There is an old saying that says, "Cleanliness is next to godliness." I would revise that to say, "The purity of worship that comes through personal pain is next to godliness." If we grow through pain and learn from it, then we experience the emotions of God Himself who sent His own Son to suffer and die and to endure the agony of the cross on our behalf. Even pain can be redemptive.

You can live in wealth and prosperity, drive a Porsche, send your kids to Harvard, never know pain, and never know God. You can't work hard all your life, suffer humiliation, know that your grandfather was a slave, and learn to live with that pain without knowing God.

Here's something else I believe strongly: All of a sudden we have large numbers of blacks who are coming into tremendous wealth and prosperity, making millions of dollars in sports, music, the media, or various other kinds of business. It occurs to me that whatever the blacks of past generations did not get through their labor, sacrifice, and strength in this great nation, their grandchildren are reaping.

So when people like Michael Jordan, Michael Jackson, Oprah Winfrey, and Tiger Woods make millions of dollars, they are simply redeeming the paychecks their parents and grandparents did not get.

If you read about what the Bible says about the woman of Shunem in 2 Kings very carefully—remember that the birth of her son was prophesied to her by God's prophet and then she eventually lost her son to death—you will see that the Bible says something very interesting. After Elisha returned her son back to life, there came a time when the famine was coming. The Lord spoke to the woman and said, "Go and find any place to live, any place, because a famine is coming."

When the famine was over seven years later she returned to her land. When she came, she went to the king to make sure that her land was given back to her. And the servant of Elisha told the king, "My lord, O king, this is the woman, and this is her son whom Elisha restored to life." Because a miracle had occurred in her life, the king gave orders to his officer, saying, "Restore all that was hers, and all the proceeds of the field from the day that she left the land until now" (2 Kings 8:6).

God is saying the same thing to black people everywhere today. It is just like the people of Israel: Their debts will be erased and their sons will be restored to them. He is saying, "I will give your income back to you. I will give it through your sons, because you are dead. The money they get is not for them. The millions they are making is not for them. It is the payback for all the wages you have not received over the long decades of pain."

If they are smart, the young people will not use the money to satisfy themselves with luxury things, mansions they may never live in, or wild parties; the money that is given them is to repay their mothers, fathers, and all their people throughout the nations. Not just this nation, but the nations of their fathers.

They need to say, "This is not just for my immediate family, but for all the people." White people need to do the same. Whites cannot use their wealth just for white people any more than blacks can use their wealth only for blacks. But it is the blacks right now who need to strive against the temptation to say, "This is just for us." They need to be wary of any tendency toward selfishness, which is of the world and of Satan, and hence, not of God.

IN TIMES OF JUBILEE

THE YOUNG BLACK people who are now reaping a harvest of wealth, fame, and fortune must stop and see what is happening. Their wealth should bless the nations. For some of them, a good start would be to help the black community—restoring broken-down neighborhoods, encouraging families who are struggling, or doing good works in their hometown. From there, they may learn to use their abundance as a blessing to the nations and to the world beyond.

I have found that the life of fame and popularity usually spans about eight years. This is a transient society. Popularity lasts for eight years. After eight years people are looking for something new. People peak, and in transient societies where the kingdom is not understood, people tend to get bored easily because there is nothing that brings them consistency.

That is why every seven or eight years people are looking for someone new. This is a society where people are used to toys. Whenever the manufacturers release a new toy, our tendency is to throw the old ones away and get a new toy. Everything is a toy.

In the Old Testament we read of the time of Jubilee, which was a year of rest to be observed every fiftieth year. By law, slaves were to be released in the year of Jubilee, property was to be restored to the original owners, and the fields were to be left fallow. God believed in blessing the people, of using our resources to bless the nation, and He taught us to set aside a time of refreshing and restoration.

Someone needs to tell the young blacks that what they are getting is not a toy. Their talent is not theirs alone; they are to serve the people. They have been gifted for the people. Think of Esther, who was instructed by her Uncle Mordecai to speak on behalf of her people, the Jews, to the king. She feared for her life, but Mordecai told her, "Who knows but that you have come to royal position for such a time as this?"

In the same way blacks need to hear this. You have been spared for such a time as this, and, thank God, you are free. Now, what will you do with that freedom? Will you remain a captive to the slave mentality? Or will you move up to a new level of independence and personal responsibility? Will you stand around and demand whatever the white man will give you? Or will you begin to use your blessings to give to others, to bless your own, and to bless all of God's people? When this becomes the focus for action, it can be one of the most liberating ideas imaginable. It can be miraculous!

What greater thing can a black man do with his money than to build a church? Not a community center, not a basketball court, but a church—a place where your people will come and give praise to their God. You see, if God gives me millions and I build a place of worship, then I give it back to God. I give Him what He desires. I would say to those who have received this world's treasure, if you first build a place to worship your King, then you can build your sports complex and your community center. The church is the place where you can give honor to God for what He has done for you.

Anytime God blessed the people of Israel, they built Him an altar. Abraham, Isaac, and Jacob built altars to the Lord. Joshua built a tabernacle at Shiloh. Nehemiah rebuilt the walls of Jerusalem so the temple could be restored. This is a message that must be heard, and not just by successful black athletes. This message must be heard by anyone God has entrusted with good fortune. If you have accumulated wealth, it is of God. You have built your business into an empire because He has prospered you. Through His favor you have received that large inheritance.

How many Christians, and how many Christian ministries for that matter, have accumulated tremendous fortunes but have not given back to God what is rightfully His? There are ministries in this country whose leaders have splendid houses, luxurious cars, private jets, ranch homes, mountain homes, beach homes, and corporate holdings that would boggle the mind. Some of them are rich beyond the dreams of avarice, while the people of God are begging bread in the streets. Can God ignore this injustice? Do you honestly think He will look the other way simply because wealth is amassed in the name of God?

All Buddhist and Muslim millionaires consider it their greatest honor to be able to build a temple of worship and to fill it with gold, jewels, and precious ornaments so their god will be pleased with them. The best thing God's people can give God is a place where people will come to worship their King. God gave America wealth so she could build Him a sanctuary.

Hear the words of David, who said, "How can I live in a paneled house when the ark of the Lord does not have a place to rest?" He told his son Solomon, "I have blood on my hands, and I may not be able to build it, but I'm going to provide you with all the means. I want you to call all the people together and build a splendid sanctuary unto the Lord." When the sanctuary was built, the Bible says the glory of God came, and He took over the temple. That day the priests could not perform their duties.

God had told the people of Israel, "I have lived in tents and tabernacles, but now I want you to build me a house." He had given them the resources when they left Egypt. The golden calf that Aaron made, however, became a hindrance. God did not trust Aaron, because he wanted temporal satisfaction. Joshua, on the other hand, was looking for eternal fulfillment. Consequently, though Aaron was Moses' older brother, Joshua, who did not belong to the inheritance, inherited the strength and wisdom. Moses laid hands on him and Caleb, whose spirit was for the future. Caleb said, "I've waited all these years, and now look, I'm eighty-something years old. I've waited forty years since the promise was given, and now I'm well able to receive it. Give me that mountain!" That was the same mountain that was promised his daughters.

If God is giving us wealth, He is giving it so we can build something for Him with which He will be pleased. When the Israelites left Egypt, how was it that they were able to bring earrings, diamonds, gold, and purple? Because God allowed them to gather great wealth in Egypt so they could build Him a home. However, Aaron took the gold that had been accumulated to build God a temple and built a golden calf to worship. Not Jehovah God, but a pagan idol!

They didn't need gold in the wilderness; it was strictly for God. But the people gave up their gold, and turned away from the God who had spared their lives. They threw themselves down before a false god. Jehovah God was furious with them. When Moses returned from the mountain with the tablets on which God had written the Ten Commandments, he was outraged also; he threw the tablets down and broke them in his anger at Aaron and the people of Israel.

BUILDING THE KINGDOM

THE WEALTH THAT God gives us is to be used to build the kingdom of God. If we seek first the kingdom of God and His righteousness, as Matthew 6:33 tells us, all these other things will be added unto us. This is such an important promise. If we take care of first things first, making sure we put God ahead of everything else, then all these other things will take care of themselves, naturally and in their proper time and place.

That does not mean that if we put on our holy face and go around saying, "Bless you, brother," to everyone we meet, that God is going to dump a whole load of riches in our lap. It means that when God comes first in our hearts and when we sincerely seek the kingdom of God, doing those things that we know He has commanded us to do, then we establish a system of order and balance and priority that will bring good things into our lives, including all the things that we need to live each day. This is not a mystery. It is simply God's system of order.

Jesus made a very powerful promise when He told us, "Ask, and it will be given to you; seek, and you will find; knock, and the door will be opened to you" (Matt. 7:7). Ask, seek, knock. He continues, "For everyone who asks receives, and he who seeks finds, and to him who knocks it will be opened" (v. 8). The Western world only knows the asking part. We don't really understand the seeking or knocking parts. "In Your presence is fullness of joy," David says; "at Your right hand are pleasures forevermore" (Ps. 16:11). The joy of the Lord is our strength, but that strength does not come if we don't seek for it.

God wants us to do more than ask. Have you ever noticed what you get when you put together the first letters of these three words: Ask, Seek, Knock? It creates an acronym—ASK. Ask God for anointing, and He will give you anointing. Ask Him for wisdom, and He will give it to you.

Whatever you ask believing, Jesus assured us, we receive (Matt. 21:22). But we must ask correctly. If we ask "amiss, that ye may consume it upon your lusts," as James 4:3 in the King James Version states, God will not give it to you.

God wants us to seek. He is not lost, but He wants us to seek Him. Seeking God does not mean asking Him for things. To seek, we have to do more than ask. We don't have to go anywhere or do anything to ask. To seek, however, we have to get up from wherever we are and go out in search of something. Sometimes we may have to go to a place where we have never been before. We may have to seek in a place we might prefer to avoid, a place that is uncomfortable for us, but God demands it if we want our prayers to be answered. Too often the church has taught us to ask but not to seek God.

The American scientist, George Washington Carver, realized that all good things come from the Father; he once asked God to show him the secrets of His universe. Carver went on to say that his goal was that all those who learn about his work would find God as he had done. For this great black scholar, the voice of God was everywhere. He said it was like a radio station. "I love to think of nature as an unlimited broadcasting station," he said, "through which God speaks to us every hour, if we only will tune in."

The treasures of God are hidden behind closed doors. God never puts His treasures where just anybody can pick them up. There has to be a relationship. When we seek for Him with all our heart, we will find Him (Deut. 4:29). We have such promises throughout the Scriptures. When we knock, the door shall be opened unto us.

A king doesn't sleep on the throne. He sits on the throne to work. He doesn't eat on the throne either. When he sits on the throne, he issues orders and decrees; he conducts the official business of the crown. He doesn't rest there or go to the throne to have fun. The throne is a place of authority, of judgment, and of grace.

Wherever there is judgment, there must also be grace and mercy. When the king sits on the throne, he is ready to execute judgment, render mercy, and reveal his hand of righteousness. But there is something else that is very interesting about the throne room: The king doesn't enter the throne room through the same doors that others enter.

The throne room is entered through a public door from the waiting room. The king's door is behind the throne; he enters the room through the inner chamber. He has a private access through which only he, his servants, and closest friends may enter.

Often the king will already be sitting on the throne before we enter. The king is never surprised by our entrance. No one ever comes into his presence without his permission. We experience the awesomeness of the king the moment we enter his presence. If he comes in while we are waiting, we rise and then bow to express our submission to the king, to praise him, or to worship him. When he instructs us to sit, we sit below the king; we never sit higher. In fact, the highest place we can sit is at the feet of the king.

Furthermore, a king never tells his secrets on the throne; he only brings forth justice, righteousness, mercy, grace, and expression of his power as monarch and ruler. When he is on the throne, he represents majesty and power. If he wants to tell his secrets, he will first go to his inner chamber.

Think, for example, of the story of Hezekiah, who took the enemy officers from Babylon into his chambers and showed them all of his treasures. He boasted about his riches to the scouts of a foreign army. In his pride, he showed them everything, every golden vessel, every shield and sword and crown of jewels in his royal treasury. The prophet Isaiah was shocked that the king had revealed his secrets to foreigners.

> And he said, "What have they seen in your house?" So Hezekiah answered, "They have seen all that is in my house; there is nothing among my treasures that I have not shown them."
>
> —2 KINGS 20:15

Immediately, Isaiah realized what had happened. He knew that the king had compromised the people and that the armies of Babylon would soon come and take away the treasures and plunder the nation of Israel, taking them away into captivity. So he said to the king, "Hear the word of the Lord," and he pronounced the following curse:

> "Behold, the days are coming when all that is in your house, and what your fathers have accumulated until this day, shall be carried to Babylon; nothing shall be left," says the LORD. "And they shall take away some of your sons who will descend from you, whom you will beget; and they shall be eunuchs in the palace of the king of Babylon."
>
> —2 KINGS 20:17–18

As we know, the prophecy came true just as the prophet said. Why? Because the secrets of the king are reserved for the allies of the king. They are not to be shared with strangers. The princes of Babylon had come only to flatter the king, to talk him into revealing his strength, and to trick him into showing where his treasures were hidden. But Solomon warned that "pride goes before destruction, and a haughty spirit before a fall" (Prov. 16:18). It all came to pass as the prophet had said. Pride destroyed the nation and the king.

But how have we changed? In our own kingdom we expose our strengths and our treasures to the alien, then we are surprised when the enemy comes, destroys our fortress, and carries away the things we possess.

More Than Conquerors

THE BIBLE TELLS US, "The secret of the LORD is with those who fear Him, and He will show them His covenant" (Ps. 25:14).

It is a privilege to be in the presence of the King. The treasures of God are behind closed doors, and unless the King takes us there, we will not know the secrets of His kingdom.

God first reveals His secrets to His servants, the prophets. Whatever the King reveals to His servants in the darkness of the inner chamber, He expects us to share with others in the light of day.

Jesus said, "For there is nothing covered that will not be revealed, nor hidden that will not be known. Therefore whatever you have spoken in the dark will be heard in the light, and what you have spoken in the ear in inner rooms will be proclaimed on the housetops" (Luke 12:2–3). We are to declare to the whole world what the King has declared to us in our private audience with Him.

As God's servants, we must first of all develop our relationships with God so that He will bring us into His inner chamber where He can reveal the secrets of His kingdom to us. Then as we begin to proclaim the glory of His kingdom to the world, we will help Him establish His kingdom in our world today. In turn, His power and glory grows. Show me a king and I will show you his power and glory, for they are not hidden. If you have no power, you are not a king. Without glory, you have no credibility as a ruler.

When Saul lost his glory, he lost his power. Meanwhile, David grew in power. When the glory was transferred to him, not only did David gain the power of the throne, but suddenly Saul no longer had a place. He had lost authority, and he soon lost his throne.

I Have Seen the Kingdom

God's power and glory are shown forth to the world of darkness by a people who are living under the authority and command of our King. We are liberated people—but the very freedoms we have been given by our King have bound us to Him in a covenant based upon His authority and our obedience.

Jesus came to set us free, but He said that the truth would set us free (John 8:32). He is the Truth, the Way, and the Life, but when we look at the way we live, who can claim to truly be free? We are in bondage to the kingdom of this world; when people are not free, their yokes need to be broken.

We are liberated in terms of the politically correct ideas of the world, but we are yet slaves. Until we willingly take the yoke of the Lord upon us, which is light, we will never escape the bonds of this world; we will always be victims of man's justice, which is the opposite of God's righteousness.

Only God can set us free, and only a life-changing faith in Jesus Christ can transform slaves into conquerors.

10

If We Love One Another

Kingdom living is a special kind of life. It may not make sense by the standards of today's world, because a kingdom principle says that giving is better than receiving. Kingdom living says that we should turn the other cheek when we're offended and refuse to fight when we're provoked—no matter how belligerent or intolerant the other person may be. That's not how the world sees it. They call that kind of behavior stupidity, but God calls it the fruit of the Spirit. It's a key principle of kingdom living.

Through the last several chapters we've examined many aspects of kingdom living; we've seen the good, the bad, and the ugly. We've seen what we should do, and we've also seen some of the things we should not do as kingdom citizens. But how do we know when we're living in the kingdom of God? How do we recognize it? What are the signs and characteristics of kingdom life?

Read 1 Corinthians 13, the great love chapter. There, in thirteen short but powerful verses, is one of the greatest love poems ever written. With every word—in verse after verse and image after image—the apostle calculates the height, breadth, and depth of the Christian life; he defines the essence of faith as love. In that chapter he calls every citizen of the kingdom to love one another, even as God loves us.

Love is the central message of the kingdom: "Though I speak with the tongues of men and of angels, but have not love, I have become sounding brass or a clanging cymbal." You immediately sense the passion in Paul's words. He is not against good works; he's all for them. He's not against evangelism; he was the first great evangelist. He is not against the manifestations of the Spirit; he's all for them, too. But the essential background to everything else, he says, is love. And his words are compelling.

He continues, "Though I have the gift of prophecy, and understand all mysteries and all knowledge, and though I have all faith, so that I could remove mountains, but have not love, I am nothing." Here is the fruit of what we've been learning as we've observed our Lord building His kingdom among the nations. He is seeking a people who are educated, challenged, and disciplined in the art of love. Not love as the world knows the word, but true love, as Christ demonstrated it by His loving sacrifice at Calvary. "And now abide faith, hope, love, these three," says Paul, "but the greatest of these is love" (1 Cor. 13:1–2, 13).

When Paul wanted to preach the gospel to the pagans in ancient Greece, he went up to their great marble temple on Mars Hill and addressed the leaders at the Areopagus. He said he had come to tell them of the "unknown God," and he described a God of majesty and power who was, nevertheless, a God of compassion and love.

> God, who made the world and everything in it, since He is Lord of heaven and earth, does not dwell in temples made with hands. Nor is He worshiped with men's hands, as though He needed anything, since He gives to all life, breath, and all things. And He has made from one blood every nation of men to dwell on all the face of the earth, and has determined their preappointed times and the boundaries of their dwellings, so that they should seek the Lord, in the hope that they might grope for Him and find Him, though He is not far from each one of us.
>
> —ACTS 17:24–27

God does not need temples built by hand, and He doesn't inhabit temples made by religious people for their own self-gratification. He resides within us and lives in our hearts. God doesn't need what we can do for Him; He's not dependent on us. He can get along very well without us. Rather, He gives us the privilege of serving Him and serving one another in love. That's how He builds His kingdom, by sending messengers, by calling them, and then by seeing who is equipped and capable of service. God determines the times set for each of us and the exact places where we should live. Why? So that we can be fruitful and inherit the kingdom.

THE KINGDOM OF HIS LOVE

TIME AFTER TIME, Jesus taught His followers how to love one another. He taught them in sermons and by example. You may remember that He put the question to a young lawyer who had asked what he needed to do to be saved. Jesus responded, "What is written in the law? What is your reading of it?"

The young man answered, "You shall love the LORD your God with all your heart, with all your soul, with all your strength, and with all your mind, and your neighbor as yourself." Jesus must have been impressed. The lawyer hit the nail on the head. So Jesus said, "You have answered rightly; do this and you will live" (Luke 10:26–28). Again, the key word is *love*. Love the Lord; love your neighbors.

God made each of us what He wanted us to be, and He placed us in many different parts of the world. He did this so that all nations might come to know Him and participate in His kingdom. God did not limit His blessings to the church in America. I know this may come as a surprise to some of you, but God actually sent the message of Redemption to people all around the globe, in every nation, and on every continent. He is not willing that any should perish but that all should come to repentance. He is calling people everywhere to the marriage feast of His Son.

Some parts of the world have never heard the names Billy Graham, Pat Robertson, Luis Palau, Kathryn Kuhlman, or Benny Hinn. They've never heard of Kingsley Fletcher, and some don't even know the names Jim Bakker or Jimmy Swaggart. They've never heard of Reinhard Bonnke or any of the other pastors and teachers we know so much about in this country. But there are men and women who know the name of Jesus Christ and worship Father, Son, and Holy Ghost in mud huts and grass shacks around the globe.

I Have Seen the Kingdom

There are hundreds of millions of Chinese Christians behind the Bamboo Curtain in Communist China. In Nepal, Tibet, Turkmenistan, and even Iraq, there are men and women who know Jesus as well as we do and who have given up a great deal more than we have to serve Him. We need to know that God is seeking people who will love Him passionately, selflessly, and with determination. That's why He allows us to endure hardships.

The Spirit of God will not linger where people have grown cold and complacent about their faith. The reason God brought your founding fathers to this continent in the first place was because England was dying. The British Empire has been dying for most of the last hundred years. Its colonies and possessions have revolted. Its territories and dependencies have cut loose the fetters of commonwealth, and even the contiguous nations of Ireland, Scotland, and Wales are demanding independence.

Spiritually, the British Empire began to crumble as far back as the English Civil War in the mid-seventeenth century. Later, under the influence of Fabians, Utopians, and Socialists in the nineteenth century—people who hated God and wanted to establish their own kingdoms in defiance of God—British Christianity virtually collapsed. By the end of the twentieth century, Great Britain is in spiritual rigor mortis. For all practical purposes, the faith of your forefathers is dead there, and the torch of faith has passed to other hands.

Whatever God does, He does with purpose. He gives people every opportunity to turn away from sin and kneel before the cross of Jesus Christ. He is not above begging them to come, but He sets a time limit on the offer. He allows His servants to endure hardships, to suffer humiliation, and to pass through the flames of death to spread the Word to the ends of the earth. God has tried everything to convince us of His love. No tricks. No lies. No fun and games. His name is Truth, and He speaks only the truth. However, He will not linger where there is no love. When the hearts of the people grow cold, He removes His lampstand from the temple. Remember Peter's words of warning?

> But the day of the Lord will come as a thief in the night, in
> which the heavens will pass away with a great noise, and the

elements will melt with fervent heat; both the earth and the works that are in it will be burned up. Therefore, since all these things will be dissolved, what manner of persons ought you to be in holy conduct and godliness, looking for and hastening the coming of the day of God, because of which the heavens will be dissolved, being on fire, and the elements will melt with fervent heat? Nevertheless we, according to His promise, look for new heavens and a new earth in which righteousness dwells. Therefore, beloved, looking forward to these things, be diligent to be found by Him in peace, without spot and blameless; and consider that the longsuffering of our Lord is salvation.

—2 PETER 3:10–15

Those who suffer and die for proclaiming the Word of God are not failures as some may think. They will receive a martyr's reward, and in the kingdom of heaven they will stand in the presence of God. But those who have heard the truth and rejected it will suffer judgment. Those who believed but failed to live with passion will also be judged; Jesus warns those whose faith is only lukewarm that He will vomit them out of His mouth. Does that seem to contradict the message that God is love? Not at all. God's love is perfect, but His limits are clear. If any man spends eternity in the lake of fire, it will be because he devoted himself to a kingdom other than the kingdom of Christ.

Wherever there is a kingdom, there must be authority. Jesus is the Lord and King of our lives. We are to take our instructions from Him, and if He says, "Come unto me, all ye that labor and are heavy laden, and I will give you rest," He does not mean that we are free to go our own way and do whatever we please. If He tells us to "go and make disciples of all nations," then it is our job, as the old Negro spiritual declares, to "go tell it on the mountain—over the hill and everywhere."

We have no excuse for disobedience to our King. Any idea that is contrary to the will of God is counterproductive and dangerous. I am a child of Africa. I found Jesus in a village more than four thousand miles from your shores. But I am excited to know that Christ has come to establish God's kingdom in my heart. I am delighted to know that He can use my skills, however limited they may be. I am also committed to go into the world and take the news of Christ's love, because I'm convinced that's what the Father has called me to do. I wouldn't think of doing anything else.

REVIVAL AND RENEWAL

PEOPLE TALK A LOT about revival in this country. We have a feeling that revival is coming—it has to come—and we think we know how it's going to come. To the thinking of many in the West, revival is going to come through the American church. I've heard pastors say, "Thank God, revival is going to come from America!" But wait a minute! Who told you so? What makes you believe that? I have to ask: Why would God bring revival from a nation that hasn't acknowledged His kingship? Why would He establish His kingdom in a land that hasn't even welcomed Him as King?

Revival may come to America—I pray it will, and soon—but if it does, it will come this way: God is going to revive a sleeping and dead church, and once we are awake, there must be growth. We must exhibit the fruits of the kingdom, and we must show by our fruits that we comprehend the meaning of Christian love. Revival is not the end of anything, as many seem to think. It's just the beginning.

Revival is happening in many countries of our world today. But we don't see it happening here, so we don't believe it.

We believe it must have our seal of approval. There are some people who look at the missions work in Korea and other countries and wonder why many Asian churches are sending Christian missionaries to America. Why are they surprised? It's no secret that America has become a deeply immoral nation. Believers all around the world weep for us, because they can see that we've fallen so far so fast. We're not the shining city on a hill we used to be.

We cluck our tongues when Asian and African missionaries come here, as if the sophisticated, democratic, technologically advanced people of the West do not need missionaries and prophets preaching the message of God's kingdom—as if we don't need revival. We desperately need revival, but until we fall on our faces and confess our sins before our King—individually, corporately, and nationally—revival will not and cannot come.

Back in 1983, while I was still living in England, God laid a message on my heart. He told me to come to America as a missionary. I didn't know a soul in this country. My wife, whom I had met and married in Mexico, came with me, not knowing a soul. But God sent us here as missionaries. Sometimes I would ask, "What am I doing here?"

God would say to me, "Son, I have sent you to teach these people about My kingdom." Our lives were stressful and uncertain during those years, but I knew I was under obligation to carry out my calling. For one thing, I know that one day I will appear before Christ at the judgment seat of the Lamb, and I'm determined to be found faithful. I want the security of knowing that I've done my part; so when God calls, I'll do whatever He tells me to do. By the time I was twenty-five years old I had lived in thirty-two countries and planted over two hundred churches. I'm not a bishop, and I don't like that title; I'm not an apostle, and I don't like that one either. I am just a servant of my King! I rejoice in serving my King, and that's my full-time job.

Beyond my own insecurities, this calling has also been a challenge for my family. I am my father's heir, and I'm expected to succeed him as chief and king in Ghana. The calling to preach the Word raised questions among the members of my family. I know they have tremendous respect for me, but they also have expectations for me. My father said to me a few years ago, "Son, because of my obligations, there are some things I have not done. It is partly disobedience and partly because of my other obligations. But I am going to bless you." And he did.

My father is a twin, and both brothers, my father and my uncle, sat me down one day, laid hands on me, and imparted the blessings of their generation and a hundred generations of our family to me. They said, "We bless you, and we break every curse that has been in our family through all the generations." That was a very moving experience. It may help to know that in my country being a twin makes you very special. It has profound mystical significance, especially if one of those twins is a king.

I Have Seen the Kingdom

To be standing there at that moment, between these twins who were laying hands on me and praying for my success (which they had never done for anyone else in our family), was a very special and stirring moment in my life. This was the blessing their father (my grandfather, the king) had placed on them many years ago. Both were Christians, and they served the Lord. They anointed me for my work. Since that time, my uncle has died. Four months after he prayed for me, he went to be with the Lord. You can imagine how I feel today, knowing that I received the blessing from their hands.

I will never forget the words of my father's blessing. He said, "Son, where I did not go, you will go. What I did not do, you will do. And what I did not speak, God will speak it through you." I cannot begin to tell you what a humbling experience it was. I have been blessed by my father, the king. I received the impartation of my father's promise. I have received his inheritance and his love. Obviously, I am indebted to him for life.

I've had the privilege of sitting with my father. I have also had the privilege of taking my oldest daughter to meet my family on two occasions, when she was seven years old and again when she was eleven. I took her to the places where I grew up, where I was born, where I went to school. In each place I would tell her about my life and my heritage as the son of the king. In the spring of 1997, I took both my daughters with me. The older child was twelve, and the younger was ten at the time. That was a wonderful experience.

My mother visited me in this country, but before my father's time is up, and before he goes to be with the Lord, I want to take my family to be blessed by both my parents. According to our tradition, my father will say to me, "Son, come and build me a home, and let me sleep in it before I die."

That is my duty, and I take the traditions of my people very seriously. I will build my father a home with my own hands. That is very important culturally, and it is symbolic to our people.

A Son's Legacy

MY FATHER IS called Jacob, and when I pray to the God of Jacob I'm not just thinking about Jacob, the son of Isaac and grandson of

Abraham in the Bible. I think especially of my own father, Jacob, because he was the one who introduced me to faith in God. My parents and family have tremendous love for me. They call me their Joseph. That's because I have been called from Africa to go to another land.

God has given me, a child of Africa, the chance to speak to the nations and to call them to repentance. If my mission to America were to fail, I would fail thousands of people in Africa who love me and who are praying for me at this moment. I am their Joseph.

My father said to me as I was leaving to come here, "We may lose a son, but we will gain children we will not live to see. We release you back to God." My oldest sister came to this country several years ago and moved to Richmond, Virginia. Recently she felt God was calling her to North Carolina, and she was able to move a little closer to me and my family.

I began serving the Lord very early, and I knew I was called to full-time ministry by the time I was seven years old. By age ten I was full of conviction about what God would have me to do, and the things I am doing today are the things that came into my heart when I was a child. I have not deviated from that vision on a single point. I love Jesus Christ with all my heart, not just because He saved me, but because He has given me a life in His kingdom.

Since I've been in America, I've been deeply concerned about the condition of many of the churches here. Image is such a big thing to them, and if anything threatens their image or their sense of security they reject it out of hand. Many churches don't like confrontation and change. Unfortunately, truth always confronts, truth reveals, and truth demands change. Truth can only set you free if you accept it as truth; we must be willing to take God's truth at face value.

It's true that the church is taking a lot of heat these days. Pastors, teachers, and authors are addressing many complex issues of our day and saying that a large part of the problem is that the church has failed to do what she has been called to do. Too often, Christians who should know better have compromised with the values of the world. They've turned their heads while the world continues in sin; they have not been salt or light in the world. We run from controversy, and in our flight we cede the field of battle to our adversaries.

One of the main reasons this is happening is because we don't understand the kingdom of God. Through our limited understanding of the kingdom and our lack of knowledge of the language of the culture in which the Bible was written, we've failed to pass on many kingdom principles. As a result, we create our own problems, and then we spend years trying to fix them.

Every believer has a duty to be involved politically. That's an aspect of good citizenship. But we need to know that, beyond our general duties as citizens, God holds us responsible for the problems in the world today. This is a principle that is taught in both the Old and New Testaments. God says, "If My people who are called by My name will humble themselves, and pray and seek My face, and turn from their wicked ways, then I will hear from heaven, and will forgive their sin and heal their land" (2 Chron. 7:14). He does not say if the government will pray, or if you get enough signatures on a petition, or anything of the kind. The burden is on God's people. Notice that the next verse says, "Now My eyes will be open and My ears attentive to prayer made in this place" (v. 15). Believers must act; we must pray. The burden is on us.

Have we fasted? Have we truly humbled ourselves before God? Have we prayed diligently and sought the face of God? Have we turned from our wicked ways? Show me how much the church has fasted and how much she has prayed, and I will show you how God is beginning to answer her prayers. This is not a weak promise of God; it is a promise with tremendous power and certainty. If we are not seeing the hand of God moving in our land today, there is only one place to look. God has not changed; He is always faithful. He is always the same. Don't look at Him, don't look at Washington. Look at the church.

I feel sorry for preachers who, because of their political persuasions, are attacking the leaders they've put into office. Do you know what they are doing? They're trying to say that they were foolish. They didn't follow God's guidance in selecting and electing public servants; they're admitting that they have poor powers of discernment. They didn't know how to pray. They didn't have the discipline to find leaders who were worthy.

This is one more sign that we don't understand the kingdom of God, for the way we treat our politicians is the way we treat our King. The Bible says we are to honor those in authority, but we don't know how to honor authority in this country. No wonder our teenagers have no respect for their parents or teachers. They have never seen us show respect for those in authority over us. If we don't show respect for our political leaders, how can we expect our children to show respect for us? They don't respect their parents, and they have no regard for their ministers.

Most of the people in government claim to go to church. If that's the case, then there's another area where the church has failed. The man or woman who is making bad policies has a pastor. That pastor is supposed to lead the congregation and teach principles of righteousness and wisdom based on the Bible. Hebrews 4:12 says, "For the word of God is living and active. Sharper than any double-edged sword, it penetrates even to dividing soul and spirit, joints and marrow; it judges the thoughts and attitudes of the heart" (NIV). If those in leadership are leading us to wickedness instead of righteousness, then clearly they are not being taught by the Word of God. So all our problems come back to the church, and, I'm sorry to say, the church has failed.

THE GREAT DIVORCE

WE CRITICIZE OUR politicians, but do we have their replacements? Have we trained up godly men and women to lead us back to God's truth? Will we have a new generation of young men and women coming up in the next few years who will speak the truth in love and challenge this nation to come to repentance? Have we put our money to work in the schools and seminaries? Have we supported our children and our young people and encouraged them to enter the ministry? If we are not doing these things, then we are nothing but sounding gongs and clanging cymbals.

Think what Jesus was saying when He gave us the Great Commission. He said, "Go therefore and make disciples of all the nations" (Matt. 28:18–19). Notice that He says "all the nations." It

193

is the responsibility of those in the church to change the world. As an African, I can attest that this is what makes the Muslims different from Christians. We have divorced religion from public life, and we are reaping the consequences of that. Muslims, on the other hand, teach that moral leadership must come from the church (or the mosque). In Iran, for example, the Ayatollah has more authority than the president. Their system is excessive, and we don't want to emulate it, but we should realize that any society divorced from moral leadership is headed for chaos.

Whether in the Middle East or in America today, the church is supposed to be the "forth-teller"—the prophet and witness of God. We are to be the prophet that God has raised to help govern the nation. A prophet doesn't condemn, but speaks about the future; he prepares other prophets to replace him. Elijah had a school for prophets, godly witnesses who hear what God is doing. The Bible says, "Surely the Sovereign Lord does nothing without revealing his plan to his servants the prophets" (Amos 3:7, NIV). Our preachers must become true prophets of God, not merely interested in building man-made kingdoms, but empassioned to proclaim the glories of God's kingdom. Then most of our problems would be resolved.

Muslims exhibit more passion for their cause than we do in the church of Jesus Christ. In the West we believe that ultimately Islam is an inadequate religion. The god of Islam is not the God of the Bible; he is a man-made god of wrath, anger, and hostility who has no resemblance to the God and Father of our Lord Jesus Christ. But those who serve the god of Islam often show more faith and devotion than we show for the God of Abraham, Isaac, and Jacob.

In my book *Catch on Fire!* I asked the question, "Where is the fire that was in you when you first got saved?" My fire has not died yet. If anything, God has fanned it into a roaring blaze. God doesn't make too many promises to us when we first come to the kingdom; He expects us to make promises to Him first. We must make a vow to Him before we can enjoy His covenant.

In that book, I was trying to wake up those within the church who are struggling with their sense of commitment and passion for God. I appreciate the church, but sometimes we have to wake up those who have a dose of apathy, because indifference will protect you from commitment. Apathy will create a haven of safety for you, and that's what it has done.

That's what's wrong with the church today. When we really put our finger on it, it's apathy. We talk about involvement, and we say "Amen, amen!" When it gets right down to it, however, most of the time we don't do a thing.

One reason for our apathy is that we have not been taught what to do; this society doesn't like for anybody to tell it what to do. We think we're liberated. The truth is that we are not free at all. Paul says, "You were bought at a price. Therefore honor God with your body" (1 Cor. 6:20, NIV). We are God's property, purchased by the blood of Christ and dedicated to His service. Because of our attitude about liberation, though, we've attempted to cut ourselves free, to sever that relationship of duty and commitment to Christ, and we have accepted another kind of bondage that is an insult to God. That's the great divorce.

Americans have been taught in the public schools for the last thirty years that the separation of church and state means we cannot incorporate our biblical knowledge into the public sphere. If we have an impulse to apply Christian principles and values to issues of our day, or if we have a godly vision for our neighborhoods, states, or nation, we are told it is inappropriate. We are expected to leave faith out of it and live our lives by so-called secular principles alone. The world is fighting us, and our nature is fighting us; we feel guilty, but we don't know how to solve it.

The Great Commission does not allow any excuses. It doesn't say, "Go and make disciples of all nations only if the world doesn't resist you, or if it doesn't cost you anything to go." It says, "Therefore go and make disciples of all nations, baptizing them in the name of the Father and of the Son and of the Holy Spirit, and teaching them to obey everything I have commanded you" (Matt. 28:19–20, NIV). We are to baptize them—the nations—and we must teach them to obey everything Jesus Christ commanded us, whatever it costs, wherever it takes us, and regardless of what difficulties and hardships it may cost us. It's that simple. The Bible says, "One Lord, one faith, one baptism; one God and Father of all, who is over all and through all and in all" (Eph. 4:5–6, NIV).

I Have Seen the Kingdom

Whenever the word *obedience* appears in Scripture, it involves a commandment, and that is what we see here. "Teaching them to obey everything I have commanded you." Then, if we obey the commandment, we have the promise that follows: "Surely I am with you always, to the very end of the age." But it is very important that we understand the conditional nature of this promise. *If* you obey, *then* I will be with you.

We do not get the privilege of the company of the Savior until we go to the nations and teach them to obey Him. That must be first. Just as in 2 Chronicles 7:14, which I cited earlier, the promise of God's blessing and forgiveness is contingent upon our obedience to His call upon our lives. How will we respond? Are we doing what He called us to do? Are we obedient to His Word and His will? That's a tough question.

How can God be with us if we do not obey? Some people are quick to cite one of the verses that promises blessings. "Therefore I tell you, whatever you ask for in prayer, believe that you have received it, and it will be yours" (Mark 11:24, NIV). Of course, such verses are absolutely true, but you will never find such a promise that is not founded upon the requirement of faithfulness and obedience. Remember that in this passage in Mark 11, the magnificent promise of answered prayer follows the miracle of the cursed fig tree. When Jesus and His disciples came upon a fig tree that was not productive (that didn't bear fruit and was of no value to Him), He cursed the tree, and immediately it withered and died.

The lesson here is clear. If we are fruitless, we will be separated from the Savior forever; if we are obedient and faithful in every circumstance, however, then we can be certain that Jesus will hear our petitions and will answer us, no matter how difficult the request may seem. Do you see the conditional nature of the promise?

This is God's pattern of answering prayer. In the Book of the Law, God says to Moses: "So if you faithfully obey the commands I am giving you today—to love the LORD your God and to serve him with all your heart and with all your soul—then I will send rain on your land in its season, both autumn and spring rains, so that you may gather in your grain, new wine and oil" (Deut. 11:13–14, NIV).

Later, Joshua blessed the people of Israel, but even in his blessing he gave them a stern warning, saying, "But be very careful to keep the commandment and the law that Moses the servant of the LORD gave you: to love the LORD your God, to walk in all his ways, to obey his commands, to hold fast to him and to serve him with all your heart and all your soul" (Josh. 22:5, NIV). Jesus said it best of all when He said, "If you love me, you will obey what I command. And I will ask the Father, and he will give you another Counselor to be with you forever—the Spirit of truth" (John 14:15–17, NIV).

Each time the promise is the same: *If* you love Me and obey, *then* I will give you.... But too often we fail to see that necessary connection. We expect God to love us without any demands, any expectation, or any response on our part. We're all for freedom and liberation so long as it costs us nothing; when it comes to responsibility, duty, and obedience, we run the other way as fast as we can.

HE WHO OBEYS

THE WILL OF God is this: "The kingdoms of this world have become the kingdoms of our Lord and of His Christ, and He shall reign forever and ever!" (Rev. 11:15). When you study the Book of Revelation, chapters 11 through 15, it can be very scary to consider what the prophet is really saying.

The faith that is talked about in the West today often places more emphasis on material prosperity than on serving God. It is a faith "to get" instead of a faith "to live." But we need to stop and reconsider what we're doing: We don't *get* by faith, we *live* by faith. Too often it's as if we have joined a club, a Christian club, and we think we've paid our dues by giving our hearts to Jesus. We have our membership cards, and we go through the membership book (the Bible) to pick out all the goodies we want from the shop. Then we think we can just name it and claim it.

To people who promulgate such a faith, I want to say, "Preacher, I want you to come with me to my village in Africa and try to preach that prosperity gospel there. We have baby demons over there that will put you to shame. Self-centered, egotistical, name-it-and-claim-it faith can only survive in America; it wouldn't last thirty seconds in my native land." I come from a place that knows what spiritual warfare is all about. I have a message, and America needs to hear what I'm saying. When I accepted Jesus, I didn't accept Him by my intellect; I accepted Him by His demonstration of power. My faith does not rest on the wisdom of this world; it rests on the wisdom of God alone.

Here is the lesson my African brothers can teach you: When you accept Christ, you must give up your idols. But let me tell you something: The idols in Africa today are really powerful. They're not trinkets and toys as many Americans think. They're dangerous demonic forces, and they can do great feats of magic. It is dark magic. Believers in my country are tested and tried by adversity, but we grow strong in faith. Far too many believers today have a faith to *get*. But we need to talk about a faith to *live*.

In Hebrews 11 we read about the great men and women of faith: Abraham, Gideon, Samson, Jeptha, David, Samuel, the prophets, and others. One thing that blesses me is that it says, "All these people were still living by faith when they died. They did not receive the things promised; they only saw them and welcomed them from a distance" (Heb. 11:13, NIV). This is the great Faith Hall of Fame. It tells of the great saints of the Bible who were distinguished by their faith, but it says that none of them received what they had been promised in their own lifetimes. Yet, they were faithful to death.

What an important lesson for us today. The Bible says, "The just shall live by faith" (Heb. 10:38). We live too much on one-way promises and too little on faith, but God has planned something better for us. We have a work to do. I have come to the conclusion that America's problems cannot be solved by Americans; they are too close to the problems. The church problem *inside* America can only be confronted by the church *outside* America. Democracy has been both wonderful and tragic for the life of faith. The democratic system in this country has allowed the common man to rise and the poor man to compete with the rich man, providing a tremendous boost to the economy both here and abroad. But on the other hand, it has been devastating to the idea of authority, for our false understanding of democracy has told us that no one may have authority over anyone else. We are all equal before the law; if we are equal, then what right does anyone else have to tell you what to do?

Democracy was a formulation of the West, but authority is a kingdom concept. Democracy is a gift and is good for our social and political life, but it doesn't have authority to dictate our spiritual life.

The English missionaries who came to Africa in the eighteenth and nineteenth centuries certainly understood the idea of the kingdom; they had lived under kings and had a political House of Lords. They had a system of nobility and hereditary rank and privilege that gave them some insight into the nature of the kingdom of God. But they did many things that undermined the work of Christ in the lives of the African people. When they came to Africa, they confused changes on the outside with the more important changes on the inside.

They thought that Christianizing the world meant that Africans should dress like Englishmen—that African men who live in the bush should wear English suits and African women should wear long dresses and carry parasols. That was ridiculous, of course, but somehow those early missionaries believed that Africans could not be saved if they lived in tribal villages and dressed as they had dressed for a thousand years. My own ancestors who lived in a hot, humid, wild, enormous, and often dangerous tropical continent were taught that they had to look, speak, think, and behave like Englishmen who live on a tiny, cold, wet island in the North Atlantic.

ABUNDANCE OF PRAISE

WHEN JESUS ENTERED Jerusalem to be recognized by His people as King of the Jews, the people rejoiced and praised Him with a loud voice. Luke says, "When he came near the place where the road goes down the Mount of Olives, the whole crowd of disciples began joyfully to praise God in loud voices for all the miracles they had seen: 'Blessed is the king who comes in the name of the Lord!' 'Peace in heaven and glory in the highest!'" (Luke 19:37–38, NIV). These are principles the people of my country have always understood.

The people who saw Jesus were excited. Jesus was the miracle worker, the Messiah, the Anointed One, and they understood this.

They cried out in joyful praise, saying, "Hosannah! Blessed is He who comes in the name of the Lord." But the religious people were upset by this. Some of the Pharisees in the crowd yelled to Jesus, "Teacher, rebuke Your disciples!"

Jesus answered them, "I tell you, if the people keep quiet, the very stones will cry out in praise" (see Luke 19:39–40, NIV). The people praised the Savior with a loud voice, with rejoicing and genuine enthusiasm. Their Redeemer had come.

We cannot praise God in silence. We cannot praise God in stately hymns. Hymns are sung in solemn gatherings to acknowledge the glory of the Lord. Praise is a spontaneous bursting forth of joy, admiration, and excitement that happens whenever the King shows up. We can't go to church without praising God. You cannot praise the King without the sound of cymbals. Segregation of worship was pioneered by the church. The church is at fault. So, today, the church is a kingdom divided. There is a kingdom of worshipers and a kingdom of praisers. God says, "No, I want it all!" God expects us to *praise* Him and to *worship* Him.

We can praise a person without worshiping him. We do that with certain athletes and celebrities. But we cannot worship the Lord without praising Him. I can praise God for what He has done for me, but I worship Him for who He is. Who are you to say that because we worship we are better than those who praise? You say that those who praise are more emotional. But how can we praise the Lord of lords and King of kings and not be emotional! If a king walks into this place, believe me, our emotions would respond! We would have to get up. Our facial expressions would change because we are in the presence of the king.

When Jesus came to the Samaritan woman in John 4, He knew that if His disciples were around they would actually distract Him from what He wanted to say to the woman. So Jesus sent the men into the village to get food. She was a Samaritan and a woman of low morals, and the Jews would have nothing to do with such a person. She had already had five husbands, and she was the pleasure of men. But Jesus struck up a conversation about water and said to her, "Serve Me." He was saying to her, "You share with Me the life you know, and I will give you abundant life." When she found out who Jesus was, not only did she leave her water pot and run back to her village, but she spread the news to everyone she met along the way.

When Jesus' disciples returned, they were shocked that their Master had been speaking to a woman of Samaria, and they said, "Master, here's some food for you to eat."

Jesus replied, "I have food to eat that you know nothing about" (John 4:32, NIV). They immediately started looking around for baskets and cups or any evidence of the meal He had eaten and didn't see it. But Jesus was operating in the Spirit! He didn't need nourishment from merely physical food—He had the nourishment of the kingdom. His meat was to do the will of Him who sent Him.

When Jesus spoke to the woman, He told her that the temple she was making such a fuss over was nothing to God. "Believe me, woman, a time is coming when you will worship the Father neither on this mountain nor in Jerusalem. . . . The true worshipers will worship the Father in spirit and truth, for they are the kind of worshipers the Father seeks" (John 4:21, 23, NIV).

We need to understand something: The kingdom of God transcends all ethnic or color boundaries. It unites the servants of the King. Are we one in the Spirit? Are we following the same Truth? If we are of one Spirit and following the same Truth, then why should we be separated? This is a very simple but powerful lesson. Paul said, "I appeal to you, brothers, in the name of our Lord Jesus Christ, that all of you agree with one another so that there may be no divisions among you and that you may be perfectly united in mind and thought" (1 Cor. 1:10, NIV). There are to be no divisions among those who love God. Jesus earnestly desired that there would be a spirit of unity among all those who believe and call upon His name.

The church's leaders are to pray without ceasing; we are to be watchmen who sound the alarm when danger is coming. We're supposed to be sitting on the wall, watching what is happening out there, prepared to offer advice, counsel, and a sense of protection to the people of God. Ministers who are the watchmen are supposed to do two things: First, they are supposed to watch, and second, they are supposed to be weeping between the porches for the sparing of their people.

Unfortunately, so many of the watchmen are so busy building their own earthly kingdoms that they neither watch nor weep; they fail time and time again to protect the flock from the dangers of the world. They fail to fall on their faces before God, weeping and interceding on behalf of the church. This is not new. It has been going on a very long time, but before God can renew us and bring us together as one body of believers He may have to seize the attention of the church. And that may be a very painful process.

Peter told the believers, "For it is time for judgment to begin with the family of God; and if it begins with us, what will the outcome be for those who do not obey the gospel of God?" (1 Pet. 4:17, NIV). Pastors and teachers will have to give an account for their leadership before God, and those of us who are concerned for the nation will have to give an account of our actions as parents, teachers, citizens, and disciples of the Lord Jesus.

Do we have power? Then why is the nation being run by godless men and women? We have access to the very power of heaven to change the direction of this nation and to put godly leaders in the place of authority. Are we doing that? If not, why not?

Every believer should seek to know the will of God and then do it with conviction. If we do, our influence will radiate out into the world; lives will be changed. That's the promise of Scripture. The challenge for the church today is to live out in daily practice what we claim to believe in principle. Let us take to heart the words of John, the apostle of love, who says, "If we love one another, God abides in us, and His love has been perfected in us" (1 John 4:12). Is that your goal? Is that your heart's desire?

Now that you've made a personal committment to seek first the kingdom of God and His righteousness, that should be your driving ambition. Why not let today be the day you begin your new walk in Christ, as a child of the King, defender of the kingdom, and heir of salvation? What greater joy could there be?

Conclusion

Thy Kingdom Come!

LET ME TELL you something that God told me. The work that He has begun, He will be faithful to complete it, and He will continue to build His kingdom until the day of His return. Christ our King began a work in us long before we came here, and that work shall go on. Nothing man can do will impede it. Nothing the devil can say will interrupt it. We can neither add to it nor take from it, because He has promised; His Word is sure.

When Jesus knew that John the Baptist was near the hour of his death, He assumed His responsibility as King to inform the people of their rights and responsibilities in the kingdom. He taught them to repent, for the kingdom is at hand. He taught them to seek first the kingdom of God and His righteousness. His purpose was to relate the kingdom of heaven to the lives of real people with real problems in a very real and complex world. And that work goes on.

Jesus said that the kingdom of heaven is like yeast that a baker has mixed into a measure of flour. It seems small and insignificant at first, but slowly and imperceptibly it percolates up through the flour to become a lump of dough. When formed, shaped, and baked in an oven, that dough becomes a loaf of bread that will nourish an entire family. But over in the mixing bowl, the original lump of dough continues to rise and grow.

Jesus said that the kingdom of heaven is like a tiny mustard seed, so small it's practically invisible in the palm of your hand. But when it's planted, the seed begins to live and grow. It sends down roots and spreads its tiny tendrils heavenward. As it draws upon the sun, wind, and rain, it flourishes to the point that it becomes one of the largest and most lavish plants in the garden. Eventually it will spread its vines like a tree and provide a dense covering of shade.

Jesus said that the kingdom of heaven is like a treasure buried in a field. When a workman discovers the treasure, he is so excited that he goes and sells all he has to buy the field that contains his prize.

Jesus said that the kingdom is like a merchant seeking beautiful pearls. When he finds one particular pearl of immense value and beauty, he sells everything to raise the funds to buy it.

Jesus said that the kingdom is like a fisherman's net that is cast into the sea to gather the treasures of the deep. It's like a sower in a field casting seed upon the earth, a king settling his accounts, and a landowner hiring laborers for his fields. Throughout the Gospels, Jesus paints portraits of the kingdom with emotional word pictures to make certain that no one will ever think the kingdom is a mere figure of speech or a pious platitude. The kingdom is real. It's ever-lasting. It's the dominion of our Father, and it's a reality in the heart of every true believer.

No Other Way

As we have traveled many miles together in these pages, we have looked at the reality of life in the kingdom of God. We've seen that the kingdom demands humility, obedience, loyalty, and commitment. Kingdom citizens are not allowed to be passive; we're to obey the edicts of our King. Our heavenly Father demands that we carry the Good News to all nations.

We have also examined the divisions within the kingdom today. We know that we're ethnically, socially, physically, and spiritually divided as never before, but we also know that Christ will not allow His servants to live that way. To serve Him and build His domain, we are supposed to strive for Christian unity and for oneness in the Spirit.

Christ expects us to advance in the kingdom. We're not to wait for some magic carpet ride to escape our worries; we're to engage in the controversy of faith, to call men and women back to the foot of the cross, and to use our kingdom values to create a better kingdom here on earth. We suffer because we have not been faithful. We've chosen weak and immoral leaders to rule us—in part, because God has given us the leaders we deserve. But we have a level of power, through prayer and participation, that the men and women of this world can only dream of. If we want to see meaningful changes in our world, then we've got to become worldchangers.

When we come to understand the nature of the kingdom, we will learn to adore, worship, and obey the King. We will have reverence for His kingdom, and we'll be anxious to serve Him. We'll want to share the Good News with others. That's how we exalt the King—by glorifying His name, by declaring His praises, and by inviting others to the marriage supper of the Lamb.

This may surprise you, but God's primary objective in sending His Son was not to save you. His primary objective was to establish His kingdom. We're not saved for the sake of being saved; we're saved so Jesus can give us new life. He saved us for the sake of His kingdom. If we live as we've been taught, we'll see our lives, churches, communities, nation, and eventually our entire world transformed. That's how we create a shining city on a hill. The kingdom of heaven is a model for us as we strive to live each day here on earth, and kingdom values infuse all things with new life.

Unless the principles we've discussed in these pages are implemented here and now by God's people and according to God's precepts, there's little hope that the nations can be restored. Politics won't do it. The economy won't do it. The United Nations and the New World Order won't do it. It won't matter if the federal budget is ever balanced; this world system cannot be renewed unless the people of God begin living out their mandate to love the Lord their God with all their heart, soul, mind, and strength, and to love their neighbors as themselves.

If the church does not change and get serious about the calling to establish the kingdom of God, then she will fail. Before revival can come to America, we will have to get our eyes back on the One who loved us and gave Himself for us. Regardless of what we do in our own strength, we're nothing without Him. If we take our eyes off Christ, then we will be working in the strength of mere men. Like Samson of old, the best we can do in our own might is to pull the whole place down on our heads.

What we need today is a better understanding of what God is preparing for us. If we understood the kingdom better, we wouldn't be able to sit at home when it's time for Bible study. We wouldn't be able to resist the urge to tell people about our Lord. We would be singing His praises and rejoicing in the power of the Holy Spirit—saving lives, healing broken bodies, caring for the lost and unlovely. We wouldn't need to call 911; we'd fall on our knees and call upon the Lord, and He would make all things new again.

We can't put Christ first in our lives, however, if we don't understand His kingdom and the rightful role of the King. I pray that as you've read through these chapters and considered all the issues in these pages, God has encouraged you and built up your understanding of these things. I pray that your heart and mind may be opened in a new way and that you may be committed to serve Him as you've never done before.

Finally, it's important that we realize that Jesus did not come into this world, primarily, to save us. He came to establish His rule and reign among men, to renew us in body, mind, and spirit, and to build an everlasting kingdom that will glorify our Father in heaven. Before He could do that, however, Jesus realized that He had to deal with His enemy, the devil. John says, "For this purpose the Son of God was manifested, that He might destroy the works of the devil" (1 John 3:8). Why should He want to destroy the works of the devil? Because the devil is trying to take over the kingdom and make it his own.

Jesus barred the way, however. He laid claim to the kingdom and chose men, women, and children as kingdom citizens. Salvation is the means He chose to accomplish this task, but salvation was never, in itself, the object of His work among men. If we really want to get into the mind of God, then we must go beyond the belief that salvation is the goal of faith. Salvation is the means by which we gain citizenship in the kingdom. It's what we do with our citizenship to glorify our Father in heaven that rejoices the heart of the King.

When we pray and our prayers are answered, we get excited and say that God has heard our requests. God says, "I'm happy you're happy, but I didn't do it for you! I did it for Me." You see, God is looking for an opportunity to show us His greatness. Whatever He does is done for the greater glory of the kingdom. He is building an eternal domain that is beyond imagination. Paul says, "Eye has not seen, nor ear heard, nor have entered into the heart of man the things which God has prepared for those who love Him" (1 Cor. 2:9). That's the Father's ultimate goal and plan.

Jesus died so that you and I, through His gift of atonement, might gain access to the kingdom and spend eternity with Him. He didn't do it so we could stop, sit down, and drop the keys of the kingdom in our pockets. He came to establish His throne and dominion, and He wants us to take our citizenship very seriously. It needs to be a full-time job.

The only way God can get us to understand the way the kingdom operates is to demonstrate His power in our lives. He has given us His Son, His written Word, and now He is saying, "Come, let us reason together." It is not His intention that any should perish but that all should come to repentance. It's His intention that all of us should spend eternity in His kingdom. That was His plan from the start. But He's not forcing anybody. He has granted us the right to choose whether or not we will come.

Have you decided how you will spend eternity? Have you decided how you will respond to the challenge and the gracious gift of the King? I hope and pray that you will make a new commitment to serve Him with all your heart, mind, soul, and strength, and that you will rededicate yourself to His commandments and love your neighbors as yourself.

As we begin to live out the kingdom life, we will be exalting our Maker and King, and as we begin to reach out to others in the name of our Lord and Savior, Jesus Christ, we will be helping to establish the kingdom that has no end.

Other Books
by Kingsley Fletcher

Prayer and Fasting
Catch on Fire
If I Were Satan

For a catalog of products or to contact Dr. Fletcher

for information about a seminar or conference,

contact:

Kingsley Fletcher Ministries
Life Community Church
P. O. Box 12017
Research Triangle Park, NC 27709-2017
Phone: 919-382-1944

Please include your prayer requests with your letters.

For more information or to receive admission materials
for the fully accredited Bible college where
Dr. Fletcher is president, contact:

North Carolina Bible College
P. O. Box 52209
Durham, NC 27717